The Sun is up, I'm vertical, it's a good day

One person's traversing
through cancer to remission

GEOFF BERMAN

BALBOA.
PRESS
A DIVISION OF HAY HOUSE

Balboa Press books may be ordered through booksellers or by contacting:

Balboa Press
A Division of Hay House
1663 Liberty Drive
Bloomington, IN 47403
www.balboapress.com
1 (877) 407-4847

Because of the dynamic nature of the Internet, any web addresses or
links contained in this book may have changed since publication and
may no longer be valid. The views expressed in this work are solely those
of the author and do not necessarily reflect the views of the publisher,
and the publisher hereby disclaims any responsibility for them.

The author of this book does not dispense medical advice or prescribe the use
of any technique as a form of treatment for physical, emotional, or medical
problems without the advice of a physician, either directly or indirectly. The
intent of the author is only to offer information of a general nature to help
you in your quest for emotional and spiritual well-being. In the event you use
any of the information in this book for yourself, which is your constitutional
right, the author and the publisher assume no responsibility for your actions.

Any people depicted in stock imagery provided by Thinkstock are models,
and such images are being used for illustrative purposes only.
Certain stock imagery © Thinkstock.

Print information available on the last page.

ISBN: 978-1-5043-2828-9 (sc)
ISBN: 978-1-5043-2829-6 (e)

Balboa Press rev. date: 3/27/2015

FOREWORD

My Story

August 2013

New chapters in our lives can bring much excitement. Some however aren't what we expected. While in the process of selling our home and buying a new one in the Desert, what I thought was a groin pull, followed by a back strain, has turned into something much more. What we know right now is I've been walking around with a mass in my abdomen. Think tennis ball or more so yes, not a friendly companion. The next step is seeing a specialist or two, which are due to happen this upcoming week and likely surgery to send the tennis ball over the fence (and not to return). From there we will take things day by day depending on what the doctors find and want me to do. And yes, for a change, I won't be controlling things.

September 2013

The disease is now known and the plan to beat it is taking shape. (Of course it was more than a doctor or two - more like six and counting.) Soon the treatment phase will begin and I can move from wondering to knowing and fighting. This phase will take some time (so I'm told) and I have no illusions of a "speedy" recovery. But recovery is what lies in store and like any other task before me in life, it too will be dealt with in the best manner possible, by me and the professionals that are gathered to help me, and with the support of family and friends the best phase will be when I'm cancer free and back to my definition of living. With treatment now underway, the outpouring of good wishes, thoughts and prayers, and as one person put it, just get better, all help to make this a manageable process. Difficult yes, but manageable. Trust me when I say it will be a joy to thank everyone IN PERSON when I'm cancer free. Until then, each day has its benefits and I know that my journey is symbolic of journeys many thousands of others have and continue to make through their lives.

We all face our demons in our own ways, some more public than others. I hope my willingness to share my trials, tribulations, setbacks and victories, is of help to each of you who read my thoughts. As I near the end of the calendar year, my journey remains incomplete, with many a mile more (treatment) to go. The battle that I hoped was a few months in duration now may run closer to a year. But the end result will remain the same - clean of cancer and a return to good health that will enable me to enjoy family, friends and work in a fuller and richer way than at the moment. January 21st marks the start of the second phase of this journey, the preparation for a stem cell transplant. This was certainly not what I had envisioned as my course of treatment but my cancer proved to be less accommodating to the chemo than the doctors or I hoped.

March 2014

Now I begin the roughly 30 day preparatory regime for the transplant and hopefully being closer to an end to my cure process. As you will see from my posts, the transplant process was delayed almost sixty days as I dealt with bacterial pneumonia. Every day seems to bring new challenges but now as the end of the first calendar quarter nears, the transplant is back on track and about to begin. While the unknown brings its own set of fears and trepidations, getting the transplant behind me will be a good thing. The transplant phase began in earnest at the end of March and as I write this, I am transplant plus six, or six days since the transplant. New and different things to address but all part of the process. Here is to continuing to the progress that gets me whole and healthy.

May 31, 2014

Remission has finally found me, after nine and a half months of this fight. It seems hard to believe that what feels like just yesterday I was told of the tumor. The road truly has been long, difficult on me and everyone close to me. But being positive with the support of family and friends, has made the fight bearable and for me, successful.

August 2014

The one-year Anniversary of my tumor being discovered is nearly upon me. Yes, much has changed in my life, mostly for the good. No, the battle to overcome cancer was not easy or fun, but it is so rewarding to have friends rally to one's aid and in so many ways I've been blessed by that support and friendship. Cancer will never again be something that happens to others; it happened to me. But I'm a lucky one - I survived and my future looks as bright as a cancer survivor's can be now over four months post my stem cell transplant.

September 15, 2014 (blog post)

Life is defined as the animate existence or period of animate existence of an individual. We measure our lives from birth to death. But it is what we experience in between that helps define us. Each phase of our life is like a chapter in a book, from newborn, toddler, school age, teenager, young and then mature adult. Our loves help bring meaning to our life but doesn't define it. We define our life.

Likewise, the difficulties we face impact us, our loved ones, our families and our friends. This past fourteen months has brought a difficulty that I can't even imagine was before me when I first felt the pain in my groin and then the doctor's call that the test results were not good. Cancer is never a word, let alone a disease, that anyone expects to visit them. I certainly never expected that type of diagnosis. But like mad Madam Mim in her sorcerer's duel with Merlin, Geoff, you've got it – Cancer.

My highs, and most of my lows, have been shared with the readers of this blog. The chapter in some ways is done as I am now "in remission". But in others, it will never be finished. Yes, I'm a cancer survivor, but I will never be the same. Friendships have been made, some strengthened, others lost. I have a new found respect for the work done by caregivers, researchers and those working to make a cancer patient's life that much better.

My life will head in whatever direction lies before me, with my return to working (a bit more than I have fortunately but with limitations) helping others deal with the pain and suffering of cancer and trying to make the most of whatever life remains now that I am cancer free.

To everyone who has taken the time to read my musings from August 2013 through this one, thank you. Your Guestbook entries, Comments, e-mails, phone calls and HUGS have made this journey so memorable and much more tolerable, that there will never be a way to thank each of you. The fact I haven't called, e-mailed or shown up on one's doorstep is not a slight on you but more a reflection of the vast number of people that reached out to help that it will take a long time to say thank you in person.

This blog isn't over by any means, but the chapter called having Cancer is fortunately closed. Ahead of me is the chapter called "Survivor". And in case you are wondering,

"The sun is up, I'm vertical and it is a (very) good day".

Your continued interest, posts, e-mails, Hugs (virtual or otherwise) and calls mean a great deal as I continue through this journey. Thanks for being a part of the journey and a part of the solution to my return to good health and the joys of living.

The above and what follows are from my CaringBridge site (www. caringbridge.org/visit/geoffberman) as I wound my way through my battle with cancer.

GEOFF

J O U R N A L

Sunday, August 25

August 25, 2013

"The sun came up and I'm upright" is the motto and its true today, so it's a good day. I'm looking forward to getting whatever this is under control. I expect to hear from Graham (my internist), who I'm seeing before the end of the day, which will help as knowing something is better than sitting on the sidelines waiting for news.

August 26th

August 26, 2013

Meeting with an oncologist and surgical oncologist tomorrow in Santa Monica after which decisions re surgery and other possible treatments will be clearer. So for now, the waiting continues, though a bit more short-term than before. And that is very manageable.

August 27th A.M.

August 27, 2013

The sun rose this morning as did I so this is a good day. Heading to Santa Monica in a few hours so there won't be much more to tell until late today. But as I start this journey, the amount of love and compassion from everyone is humbling and has made this that much more bearable.

I look forward to being able to thank everyone in person in the future and for "Dad the Voice" to be heard with much love for everyone.

Geoff (DTV)

August 27th evening

August 27, 2013

Well, I'd love to tell everyone that the day provided lots of answers but that would be far from reality. Six hours and three doctor visits later, we know about what we knew yesterday. My unwanted visitor remains firmly implanted inside of me (at least for now). Still no idea what type of tumor it is, or if its benign or malignant.

We do however have the start of the process to identify and deal with this. I get another round of doctor visits tomorrow and some sort of scan. Then it will likely be a CT guided biopsy on Thursday; home Friday. Once those are done, then a diagnosis and a protocol for dealing with it. Safe to say this will probably be a longer haul than short. That's okay if the end result is a clean bill of health.

At this point, I'm ready to decompress for the night, hurt a bit less (yes I'm being good and taking my pills as told) and get some sleep. Thank you to each and everyone for their love and support as we start down this journey. It makes it that much easier.

August 28th A.M.

August 28, 2013

We spent the morning very quietly after the best night's sleep I've had since this all began (6 + hours). Autumn and I took a nice walk - yes I'm still walking whenever I can. The schedule has been accelerated a bit as I am having the CT guided biopsy this afternoon. Once that is done and they are comfortable that I'm doing okay, we will get some dinner and head back to the Desert tomorrow so as to miss the holiday traffic.

We will have more to let everyone know about once the results of the biopsy are in and decisions about treatment are made, which will likely be next week sometime.

Thanks for the continued thoughts, prayers, hugs and support. They are most heartwarming. And yes, the sun rose this morning and I got to vertical, so it is a good day!

August 28th (Afternoon)

August 28, 2013

Nothing is as it seems. Our wonderful healthcare system makes diagnostic efforts more than difficult. I'm still waiting for approval of the scan and biopsy so the procedures have been postponed until early tomorrow morning. Nobody said getting well would be quick or easy.

So the rest of the day, it is resting, eating and drinking lots of (non-alcoholic) drinks. Once the tests are over, we will be headed home, so I would ask for some patience as the next update is not likely to be posted until tomorrow afternoon.

Again, thanks for the thoughts, prayers, hugs and wishes. They are most welcomed.

August 30th P.M.

August 30, 2013

Not much news today. Still awaiting results (likely next Tuesday-Wednesday). Today was a quiet day; breakfast out with Autumn at a diner we know in Cathedral City and a couple of errands. That was enough to send me to the couch for a couple of hours "nap" (or something like that). Needless to say I was/am a bit tired and every chance I can rest a bit to be ready for the next phase of this is a good thing, so I'm not arguing.

Thanks to all of you for your love and support.

And the sun came up today and I got vertical to go outside and enjoy it, so it's (been) a good day.

Geoff

August 31ˢᵗ - morning

August 31, 2013

We hope this finds everyone enjoying the start of the Holiday weekend. Autumn and I took a walk this morning as it was in the mid-80s. A bit humid but not too bad. We went over to the dog park and met the morning crew. Autumn got her first real dog fix since we moved here.

The view is looking through the wash behind our house and the mountains are the San Gorgonio Mountains and just part of what we like about being here.

My mom, broken arm and all is coming to visit and get some family time with Arielle and Ryan and us. It will be a nice diversion from the relatively continuous "ouch" I'm feeling. It will be nice to get this thing out of me and to get recovery underway.

Still nothing to report on my results and won't get anything until Tuesday, so we are in a quiet and rest mode. Here is a shout out to the Ohio "Tan Man". Knock them over with your smile next week. I'll follow in your footsteps shortly.

But the sun came up and as you can see, I am vertical. It's a good day!

Labor Day 2013

September 2, 2013

All's quiet on the Western Front. Had a chance to see my mom as she recovers from a broken arm (as the result of a fall) so she could see our new home. Arielle and Ryan came as well (thanks Ryan for the some assembly required assist and picture hanging as well) and had a visit from friends that really brightened up yesterday.

Really not much to report as we await results. Having not left the house now in almost three days, I may take an excursion just to see something different. Otherwise, patience and pain pills (a catchy new tune . . .) sleep when my body deems it allowable, watch some golf, etc.

May everyone's Labor Day be joyous and filled with sunshine. I've already done the vertical thing so it's a good day.

September 3ʳᵈ - Late Afternoon

September 3, 2013

Well, I'd love to tell you that I have a diagnosis, but that would be not quite true. I did hear from my lead oncologist this morning while Autumn and I were on a 2.25 mile walk (yes, I'm still keeping that up as much as possible, even if now at best its a 3.0 mph pace). He was still waiting for the report from the pathologists as to just what my tumor is, so for now a bit more awaiting.

Our home is coming together - put together a wine rack today (if only if could really enjoy a glass of wine right now) and Autumn ordered new patio furniture so when the weather cools down we can enjoy the back yard and our quiet surroundings. A few more things to order and we will take a break from those things until the dust settles.

I want to thank members of the swimming community that all of the Berman's were a part of for so many years for their caring and notes. It is truly amazing to know the extent of the people one touches in their lives. DTV lives on - and thank you.

Lastly, I know that I am very lucky as much of what I've been told is positive. I found out last week that a friend of mine, Bryan Axelrood, an estate planning lawyer in Century City lost an all too brief battle with pancreatic cancer. Our heart goes out to his family as he was both a nice person and wonderful lawyer.

That said, the sun came up and I was vertical, so it has been a good day. Thanks for caring and reading as I go through this.

GLB/DTV

Geoff Berman

September 4th - Evening

September 4, 2013

Well, the diagnosis has finally been made. I would tease and say drum roll or the envelop please but I'll spare everyone the suspense. Yes, I have a form of cancer. More directly, I have been diagnosed with a form of lymphoma. I don't have all the specifics yet, but from what I have been told so far, if I had to get cancer, this was the best form to get. Very treatable and survivable.

Autumn and I will go back to Santa Monica Friday morning for an appointment with the oncologist. There are likely a couple of more tests to be run before a treatment protocol is finalized and the tests will probably be in Santa Monica next week sometime. More on that score on Friday.

But all of my doctors, and I spoke with three of them this afternoon and this evening, say that if I had to get cancer, this was the best one to get. (Okay, I'd love to have passed on the option but that wasn't a choice I was given.)

So there you have it. I'm doing fine - Autumn and I went out to dinner with friends tonight and have started talking with family about what lies ahead. I'm told likely a bit of tough days, weeks, even months, but at the end hopefully a clean bill of health.

Yes, it has been a good day, compared to the alternatives. The sun came up and I was vertical. No tears, no why me. And now I get ready to face tomorrow, more easily with the love and support from everyone around me.

And to Ohio Tan Man, your surgery is not that far away and I expect you to get past it without any issues. Geoff

September 5ᵗʰ - Afternoon

September 5, 2013

A quiet day on almost all fronts. I have a visit with the oncologist tomorrow morning, followed by two tests before Autumn and I will get to go home. Think of it as another chance for people to poke me with needles and fill me with more radioactive "stuff". I might not need a flashlight to walk the house at night soon. I hope to learn a bit more tomorrow but will probably still be waiting results into next week.

Otherwise, I'm taking the opportunity to rest up a bit, or catch up on the sleep I don't seem to get each evening. Thanks for the continued prayers, thoughts, hugs and positive good wishes. They are a big help.

September 6ᵗʰ - Evening

September 6, 2013

Long day to/from Santa Monica. Multiple visits with the oncologist, a PET scan and a heart echo test. All passed so on to the next round. PET scan came back clear (i.e. no additional areas of involvement) and my heart is just fine.

Next week is a bone marrow aspiration (outpatient surgery and thankfully not awake for the procedure itself), followed by an appointment with a neurologist who has been added to the team. All snide comments can be kept to the author's, thank you. Then an appointment with an oncologist in the Desert and after that we start the good-bye tumor process.

All in all an encouraging day. Traffic to/from Santa Monica, taking almost 4 hours each way, is a reminder why slowing down in the Desert was something Autumn and I chose to do.

It was a good day - the sun came up, I went vertical and got good news.

September 7th - Morning

September 7, 2013

A small bit of irony in all this. The medical acronym for my form of lymphoma is "ABC" (meaning Aggressive B-Cell). As many of those of you kind enough to follow this interlude in my life, you know that in the insolvency world ABC stands for Assignment for the Benefit of Creditors, something I'm rumored to know a thing or two about. Now if the doctors only knew. . . .

The sun has risen with a beautiful sunrise and I'm up and about. It's going to be a good day.

September 8th/September 9th Morning

September 9, 2013

The chance to reach out and touch friends is a big deal, at least for me, so getting a Nancy Rapoport hug in person was a special event. I know that for many, reading this blog is a great way to know what's going on, but hearing, seeing and feeling first hand are even better. It works both ways. It was very special that after competing at the U.S. Ballroom National Championships in Orlando last week (and coming in 2nd overall in her class) Nancy would take an hour to sit down with Autumn and me while we are in Las Vegas to see Autumn's mom, who is having her own fight with (lung) cancer. And Nancy's hugs are legendary.

This week brings a bit more clarity to the fight ahead. I have the last of the diagnostic tests tomorrow and a visit with a neurologist and another oncologist. After that, the roadmap to good health should be ready for the great reveal. Like everything so far, I'm just going to take this one-day at a time. The doctors know a whole lot more than I in this regard (I know, that was a real stretch wasn't it) and I have put my trust and faith in their expertise.

The sun keeps coming up and I keep getting vertical, and with an in-person hug yesterday, it was a very good day. Thanks for the continuing support as I go through this chapter of my life. Please keep sending your thoughts, prayers, wishes and yes, hugs. They are so very appreciated.

September 11th - Evening

September 11, 2013

Well, the diagnostic phase appears to be complete. The preliminary results of my bone marrow test, done yesterday, were negative, meaning no other involvement of the cancer. This is wonderful and for us, exciting news.

The treatment phase begins this week, all things being equal (i.e. approval from the insurance company to cure me). What I know so far is chemo, so I will have a small pharmacy at the house and lots of good people supporting me through the process. The doctor and staff here in the Desert (at Desert Memorial's Comprehensive Cancer Center), were wonderful today and warm and friendly. No doubt I will have good days and bad, but I'm looking forward to being well soon (whatever soon is).

I'm also blessed with a very supportive wife, family and friends. Autumn has been through a lot these past few months and she is first at my side through this, running interference when necessary, making sure I follow directions and most important, just loving me. I'd be much poorer off in this without her. So please don't be offended when you call if she answers my phone - it means I'm working on getting better - and I'll get back to each of you.

Thank you for the continuing thoughts, prayers, hugs or however you are sending wishes my way.

September 12th - Evening

September 12, 2013

A quiet day on many fronts, though starting with the good news, the preliminary results from the bone marrow test were very good - no bone marrow involvement. This means it appears the cancer is concentrated in one place. A mellow "Yippee" as I'm a tad tired tonight.

But because the tumor remains firmly imbedded at the moment it still is sending not so gentle reminders of its presence. And no, they don't feel great. Here's to the process of sending this intruder to oblivion soon. On that front, I'm at the mercy of the insurance company (still) but that should get resolved hopefully tomorrow.

For those who are not so comfortable putting your feelings down on the Guestbook, please don't worry. Your thoughts and prayers, expressed in your own way and on your terms, are just as meaningful to me, Autumn and the rest of our family. There is no right way to deal with this and I hope everyone understands that there is no expectation on my part as to how vocal, visible or anything else you are. Again, just knowing you are out there watching, and CARING, means a great deal.

And because I may have been a bit neglect over the past couple of days, the sun came up today and I was (and am) vertical. It has been a good day.

September 14th

September 14, 2013

Treatment officially begins Monday morning bright and early. With some cajoling apparently, the insurance company has now seen it appropriate to get me back to good health (it is so very nice of them).

Patience was not quite stretching thin, but let's just say this was another test of fortitude. My thanks to the folks who were running lead on addressing the insurance issues throughout the past three plus weeks.

This weekend will be spent getting ready for treatment. Autumn and I had a flurry of activity around the house and are now working on hanging pictures, making sure the patio furniture is where we want it, etc. And there will be plenty of football and golf to take naps to.

I continue to be most thankful for the love and support I have received from all facets of my life. I am blessed to have so much love coming my way and I look forward to thanking everyone in person when I am healthy and back at my pre-cancer form of living.

The sun is coming up and I am vertical and this is a good day.

Treatments have begun! ▓▓▓▓▓▓▓▓▓▓▓▓▓▓

September 16, 2013

I'm home again after the initial portion of the first chemo session (this one is a two-parter so the doctors are comfortable as to how I'm handling the Rituxan (the "R" in the RCHOP protocol). I go back for the second part of this first dose tomorrow morning.

The staff at the Comprehensive Cancer Center in Palm Springs are fabulous. For people dealing with life altering disease for people and rarely seeing a patient at their finest moments, they really express care, compassion and loving treatment. Today was much more pleasant than I could have ever imagined or expected.

I won't kid and say that was a piece of cake. I did manage to sleep through about 2/3rds of the better part of the six hours (on and off of course), but sleep is sleep at this point. A bit less pain, the love of Autumn by my side and I'm feeling even better about batting this tumor into oblivion and getting back to good health. It will take some months, but that's okay for the end result.

So again today, I can say unequivocally the sun rose this morning, I am vertical and it is a good day. Thanks for caring and following as I wind my way through this journey.

September 17th ▓▓▓▓▓▓▓▓▓▓▓▓▓▓

September 17, 2013

I have officially completed the first chemo treatment. Now if someone could give me the license plates (yes plural) of the convoy that ran me over somewhere down the road I may catch up with them. In the meantime, I'm very glad the distance from the Cancer Center to the house is not that far at all. I got home today to immediately go down for a 90 minute sleep (no, I can't call it a nap). Whatever it was, it was very necessary.

I'm feeling okay all things considered. No, no three-mile walks in the near future but I will resume walking just as soon as I'm up to it, hopefully tomorrow or Thursday (we have an indoor track at one of our clubhouses so as to avoid the still hot days).

My next chemo session is on the 30th - enough time to recover from this one and be ready for round two. Your posts, thoughts, prayers, hugs and forms of positive vibes are greatly appreciated, not just by me, but by Autumn as she stands beside me through this.

And by my girls as well and while on that front, I can say Michelle is handling my illness pretty well (hard to have your dad get this sick and be 2000 miles from home) and Arielle and Ryan who told us that we are going to be grand parents come next April/May. Not like I needed things to live for, as I have plenty, but this is a wonderful added blessing and bonus that makes all of us beam with pride and love.

With that, the sun is up, and I'm standing tall - it is a very good day.

September 19th - Afternoon

September 19, 2013

Well, the best I can say is the day after chemo is something else. The day was spent feeling like I was on the wrong end of that large convoy - forget one truck, there had to be at least twenty that ran me over. Not that I could count them. I made it through, thanks to the drugs (yes, I'm taking everything the doctors want me to take) and Autumn's love and support, as well as everyone who keeps my spirits high with their thoughts and well wishes.

Today has been better - not great mind you, but better. Today has been more a tired, worn out day than a run over day. I started my re-conditioning program today with a half-mile of walking around the indoor track at one of the clubhouses here in our community. Where I am usually a pretty good paced walker, I was definitely the slow poke. So be it, its a start and hopefully will help my return to full health be a bit easier and maybe a day or two quicker.

I stay attuned to the goings on in the insolvency community as best I can. I know the ABI's Reform Commission is continuing its work with Bob Keach and Al Togut at the helm, and Bob, Bill Brandt among others spoke at the Miami Bar Association event last night, one I was scheduled to make. I have gotten a rain check so I can join the group the next time and look forward to continuing the Commission's efforts to bring reform to the world of Chapter 11.

Much past that there isn't. I've become a good mid-day sleeper (by design or enforced, it doesn't matter). Now its regain a bit of strength to get ready for chemo round two a week from Monday.

Thanks for staying up with me as I travel this very unknown road.

September 21 (Early A.M.)

September 21, 2013

Yesterday was the best day post chemo this week - a good starting point for this update. I was able to get quite a bit done around the house and for the first time since we moved in, there isn't an opened and empty moving box to be seen. Our garage hasn't looked this good ever! The day ended with a nice meet and greet mixer in our community and it was great to connect with people in a similar "new resident" state as we have been. And as is no surprise in a senior community, there many cancer survivors here so I am just one of many, a comforting thought during those less than good days (yes those do happen every now and then).

With this process seems to come an almost daily change in how I feel. I got through the day without the aid of an inter-day snooze (okay, crash and burn but who's counting) but the night has been meet with two short sleep sessions and a now couple hours wide awake, brain engaged, period. Just when I thought a good night's sleep was upon me. Oh well, it just makes the "adventure" a bit more interesting. Maybe it's the start of Fall tomorrow and an early attempt to join the Zombie regimen. Let's hope not.

Much to look forward to this weekend including a visit with Arielle and Ryan, so we can celebrate Arielle's birthday on Sunday and a shout out my friends in the swimming world, including my friends from FAST and NOW Aquatics in Michigan where Michelle is an age group coach. Hearing from my Dad The Voice life brings many a wonderful memory and a smile to my face. The "voice" is a bit scratchy at the moment, likely a casualty of the chemo, but it will be strong again when this journey is complete.

The picture is from our recent trip to Kauai and our first ever Kayak adventure. All of us, Arielle, Ryan, his sister Leslie and Autumn included, made the trip (notice who they left to paddle alone) up the Hanalei River and then into Hanalei Bay for a snorkeling side trip and lunch. It's an experience worth taking if you get the chance (and swimming with the fishes isn't too bad either - more on that another time).

While this morning the sun has not risen yet here, please know I fully expect it to rise in the East and that I am already (though way too early) vertical. It will be a good day.

September 23rd (Morning)

September 23, 2013

A wonderful day yesterday being able to share part of Arielle's birthday. I hug from family seems to have just a wee added touch to it (not that I refuse hugs mind you). She and Ryan came out Saturday night, bringing some pictures of the little one growing inside Arielle and were able to partake in some of our slowly developing routine, including lunch with friends here in our community and a walk around the indoor track (I made it 2/3rd's of a mile this time in 30 minutes - woo hoo!).

Ryan pulled out his magic tools and helped (okay, I basically watched) hang some of the bigger pictures in my office, the charger for the golf cart, and made sure all the new dining room chairs were put together properly and were tight. It is a joy to know that our children find special people to help fulfill their lives and these two fit that mold beautifully.

I also got a series of pictures from Michelle doing her cross-fit routine. All I can say is better she than me. I was tired just looking at the pictures of her activity. Go girl is the phrase I believe.

The routine seems to be settling in as I start week two of recuperating from chemo - round 1. Every day is filled with a challenge and I frankly don't know from hour to hour if I'm going to be feeling terrible, good, great, or somewhere in-between. But the sun is up and I'm upright, so today, like yesterday, is a good day.

Thanks for staying attuned to my traverses and caring . . . .

September 24th (Afternoon)

September 24, 2013

It's been a good day today (even more so than the sun coming up and my being upright, which I am thank you). I've been able to stay off the pain pills for now almost a week (yeah!) and I think, okay I hope at least, that they have cleared out of my system. Sleep was a welcome thing last night and I probably had more sleep at one time than I've had on all but two occasions since the cancer starting making its presence known. Of course two plus months of little sleep leave me looking for more, but that I can deal with!

For those of you who have to face cancer, I read today Dr. Stephanie Carter's *"Taking Charge of Fighting Cancer"* book and CD (music and inspirational thoughts). She is an advocate of the role of positive thoughts, relaxation and attuning yourself to the power of helping oneself heal. I strongly recommend a look at this helpful and thoughtful tool to aid in one's own recovery process. Many thanks to Stephanie and her husband Francis, a long time bankruptcy lawyer in Miami, FL for sharing Stephanie's work.

With the good day comes wanting to work on things around the house as we get it more the way Autumn and I want them. The goal was aspirational, but then wobbly legs and a nap overtook me. But it has been and is good. I'm feeling a bit better heading to the next chemo session and I take that as a positive so it stays in my daily goals.

Otherwise, it is a beautiful afternoon here in the Desert, not in triple digits but warm enough that being outside right now is not a great idea, so I am happily inside. I've had the chance to talk with friends from all across the country today, which as added to the very good day and I thank them for reaching out to me. Those touches from all aspects of my life bring a warmth and healing power that rivals almost every medicinal treatment I'm going through. The photo is from our kayak/snorkeling adventure last month while in Kauai. The kooky looking one is Arielle (I'm closer to the creature from the black lagoon, but who cares, it was fun).

With that, may tomorrow be as good as today and know that the sun will rise again in the morning and I'll be up enjoying it.

September 25th - Evening 198.4

September 25, 2013

Can't really say too much for the day. It was a good day and Autumn and I just got back from dinner out, my foray out of the house for the day. The non-chemo week has its ups and downs but all things being equal, a good start to being ready for the next beat down (er chemo) session.

The big thing right now is trying to not lose too much more weight. The number at the top of the post is my weight as of this morning. I will post the current number every couple of days. When I started to lose weight on a voluntary basis I was at 231, so with the voluntary and now involuntary weight loss, I'm down over 30 pounds since May 1st. I haven't been under 200 in almost 25 years and no, I don' think I qualified for the Biggest Loser before and I certainly don't qualify as a contestant now. Don't expect to see all the pounds back on, but certainly some in the future for sure.

Otherwise a quiet day. A little work, calls with friends and helping around the house. And no nap either. Bed may be a tad early tonight, but I think I can handle that. More than two hours sleep at a time would be nice too, except that is bordering on begging, so I'll take what I get and say thank you.

With that, I'll write again after the next sunrise and my being vertical - it will be a good day.

September 26ᵗʰ Evening

September 26, 2013

A really good day with Autumn as we walked El Paseo Drive for a couple of hours and then did some shopping for things needed around the house. The temperature in the Desert was in the mid 80's and a hint of Fall was in the air. As I mentioned to a friend in an e-mail, enjoy the change in the colors and climate - take a walk with your family, enjoy the sights, sounds and smells of Fall and give and get a hug. It's a brilliant time of year and I'm happy that today was a day to be able to enjoy it here so well.

I also was able to read a bit more for work on a few things that needed some attention. It's nice to be able to contribute, even a little bit. I thought of my ABI Leadership friends as well, as they held their Executive Meeting in Alexandria, VA today in what I was told was gorgeous weather. I was there in spirit.

For the Tan Man, postponement of surgery a week just means we recuperate from our travails together next week. I've got no doubt you will tackle the surgery head on and do well. Positive vibes headed from the Left Coast.

Lest anyone think I am delusional, I know what lies ahead starting Monday is another round of getting better by getting knocked down.

Its okay as the end is worth it. A few days in there may not feel quite that well but so be it.

On a different note, I saw a glimpse of retirement in the mirror and know that I need to fill some voids. I'm working on ideas and as retirement is more than a few years away, I have time to work on these ideas.

So for the end of today, the sun was warm and I got to enjoy it - a very good day. May tomorrow be filled with more of today, for everyone reading these posts but importantly, for me.

Thanks for continuing to follow me through this journey.

September 27ᵗʰ (Evening) 201.3

September 28, 2013

Welcome to the POWER of the smoothie! Under the guise of getting more calories into me, I've been having a *loaded* smoothie every night: a Boost (drink), yogurt, ice cream or sherbet, fruit and a little chocolate something (blueberries, coffee beans, M&M's etc.) and see, a couple of pounds added back to the frame. Nothing major but I'll take the add versus the subtract.

Otherwise, a beautiful day in the Desert, which I was able to enjoy both by a trip out and about, as well as sitting on our patio or lanai if we were in the Islands, a bit of coolness creeping into the evenings and then enjoying some quiet time.

I'm not sure what the weekend holds as we tend to take things a bit more spontaneously right now based on how I feel and before round two begins. No doubt some "fun" to be had.

I'm looking forward to the sunrise and being vertical to enjoy it. . . .

September 29th Late Afternoon 201.5

September 29, 2013

It is still a bit amazing to me the speed with which change takes place in my body. After a fun morning out and a late lunch, I was run over by whatever I ate that my system chose to not like (no, I will not point fingers at the lunch spot or the food, just because I seriously doubt I can pin point the exact culprit). But what it did was wipe out my afternoon and evening and send me to an early evening in bed. Just when I thought it was safe to enjoy a day - ha!

Today has been quiet, a little football watching, some errands, fixing some outdoor solar lights in the back yard, helping put a coat of paint on a wall in our guest bathroom for a little bit of color (Arielle can guess which color too) and just dealing with things.

Tomorrow we start round two - should I say enough said. But the sun will come up and I will be vertical to/from the treatment center, so it will be a good day, and one day closer to being fully healthy again.

Thanks for continuing to stay up with my comings and goings.

September 30th Morning

September 30, 2013

Chemo, round 2. Say no more. I'll report in later. . . . . . .

October 1 - AM 203.3

October 1, 2013

For anyone that thinks lying in a bed having Alien Be Cremated (yes, another ABC reference courtesy of nurse Kristin) juice run through your veins is restful, you'd be partially right. The intravenous application is not too bad - of course courtesy of a load of Benadryl by which one sleeps through most of the day. However the convoy of trucks that runs you over while you are asleep (it must have been the same convoy from round one for a return visit) while your body immediately starts trying to fight off the invaders leaves me at least a bit weak in the knees. So today is the start of trying to get through the next couple of days and then rebuild for round three. First however is the shot to assist the regeneration of white blood cells, meaning this afternoon and evening will be a quiet and slow day.

The slow process is just that - a slow, long term process to health, so its okay. The daily changes are milestones (good and bad) but they help with being more comfortable each day that I will beat this. The picture is from yesterday (during my waking moments). Not pretty but a reminder of reality and no, you can't see how skinny I am!

The sun is up and while I'm vertical (sort of), it is and will be a good day. Here's another shout out to the Tan Man, who I hear did real well with his heart surgery and now is in the CICU in Cincinnati. To his parents and family, Autumn and I continue to send all the positive vibes we can as we go through our traverses together. Stay strong young man.

October 2nd - AM 201.9

October 2, 2013

The convoy has run its course and chemo round 2 is behind me. I'm still picking up the pieces (think Wylie Coyote after a run in with a failed attempt to catch the Road Runner). This time around has been a bit different from round one, some a bit easier. The Neulasta shot was not as debilitating, in part because of a suggestion from the nurse to take a Claritin pill before the shot - it worked, at least until the end of the day when I did get really tired. Sleep was so so, a bit disappointing to say the least.

A highlight of the day was a Cincinnati care package of Graeter's ice creams. I now have a 12 count selection of ice creams for the smoothies, though the Mint Chocolate Chip is on hold until Ryan and Arielle can come out again and have some (it is Ryan's favorite flavor after all and I don't want to disappoint him by telling him about it and then devouring it before he gets to share - that would be mean . . .).

Every day is filled with new twists and it adds to the "adventure" - well some how and some way I think. Negative thoughts are told to stay off premises and for the most part they listen, overwhelmed by all the thoughts, prayers, good wishes and hugs that have an continue my way. Please know that every one holds great meaning for me and makes each day that much easier to navigate.

As for those who suggest some creative ways to pass the time (Ted and Amy that includes you), I have things that cross my mind, but none that reach those levels of dysfunctionality (I hope).

The sun is coming up and I'm already vertical - it is a good day.

October 3rd – Afternoon

October 3, 2013

Let me start with a follow up to yesterday's post, courtesy of the "Hug Mistress" (my new name for my pal Nancy Rapoport) for sending me a link to some of the Road Runner cartoons. If you haven't looked at these in a while, click on the link and have a good laugh Enjoy! http://www.dailymotion.com/video/xgk12u_rudy-larriva-s-road-runner-cartoons_creation. It brought a needed smile to me yesterday. Hugs back to you Nancy, with love.

Now, for the concept of being a "normal" cancer patient, reality rained down right after the second chemo session on Monday, and try as I did to blame Shiloh and Dakota (our "girls/cats") for leaving their fur on the couch and my pillow, the reality was I was like most cancer patients and my hair was coming out in droves. So rather than continuing to leave fur all about, I went and had my head shaved today at the new Art of Shaving store on El Paseo Drive. The ladies in the store, Beatriz and Kimberly, were very kind and understanding and made the process a much more pleasant experience than I thought it would be. They are the ladies along side of me in the picture, and I thank them for making the new me. I have had someone already tell me I was as good looking as Yul Brenner and if so, I'm in truly wonderful company.

So today has been a full and interesting day - the sun came up and I got new experiences to add to this travail.

I'm getting used to the new look, but more importantly, it was a good day.

Thanks for continuing to care.

October 4th - Afternoon

October 4, 2013

Just a short note first with thanks to Kim and Chuck for watching over me (making sure I don't keel over to be more exact) while Autumn goes to a family wedding in New Orleans. Her day was much worse than mine due to snow in Denver and the resulting travel nightmares of weather.

I worked a bit more than expected today to help with some possible new work - all good but now more than a bit tired. Nice to keep the brain engaged but it too needs a rest. I'm getting used to the bald look - the feel is still a bit new thank you. The ponytail idea *is not mine thank you* nor will there be any mullet! I'll just get used to the new me for a few days.

Otherwise, with the sun up, a beautiful day in the Desert and being upright and a bit busy, it's been a good day.

October 6th - AM

October 6, 2013

Patterns throughout this adventure aren't always what we think or expect. As I turn the corner on the second round of chemo and into the (hopefully) gather strength week before round three, some of what I expected this past week didn't come to pass. Highest on that was my sleep pattern. While I won't say sleep is over-rated, some might be nice. During one of my early morning laying awake periods, the words from Garth Brooks' song "If Tomorrow Never Comes" came into my head - and not in a melancholy or negative way.

> "So tell that someone that you love
> Just what you're thinking of
> If tomorrow never comes"

It reminds me that what I am going through is something that can't be done alone and without the love and support of my wife, my friends and colleagues, this would be an incredibly more difficult journey to complete successfully than I otherwise face. To friends who continue to reach out to me, you are a ray of sunshine to brighten the days; to friends who stop by and like Kim and Chuck who made sure nothing happened to me this weekend, my deepest gratitude (and no, I did not expect an issue but was glad to have someone watching over me while Autumn got to go to a family wedding in New Orleans); to our girls, my mother and sister who listen and read my almost daily musings, likely with a snicker and smile or two; and to Autumn, whose strength knows no bounds, whose love is immense and who makes this so much more manageable than it would be without her.

29

For me, tomorrow won't "never come", at least for a long, long time I hope. So I wanted to be sure to let Autumn, and everyone else know "Just what I was thinking of".

The sun is up, I'm vertical, and it is a good day.

October 7ᵗʰ - AM 201.3

October 7, 2013

I had the pleasure of seeing Paulette and Bill Albertson yesterday on their way back to the Tucson area after their trip to Anaheim and family time. Paulette was the wonderful lady who was my secretary for over 12 years through part of my CMA and my early DSI years. She and her husband have had their battles throughout, including Bill's now almost nine-year fight with Leukemia. Paulette looks great, having lost a good deal of weight and been able to keep it off for a few years now. Retirement has treated them well and that they would stop on their way back to Tucson to spend an hour with me brightened up my day immensely.

Arielle raised an interesting song for me to think about today - Tim McGraw's "Live Like You Were Dying". First, let me stay that *I am not dying - period*, at least not anytime soon thank you. But the lyrics made me think a bit.

> "Like tomorrow was a gift ..
> To think about what you'd do with it.
> I went two point seven seconds on a bull named
> Fu Man Chu.
> And then I loved deeper and I spoke sweeter

Every day is precious and when we take a moment to look, we can find all sorts of joys to fill and enrich our lives. I can't say I will ever sky dive and that's okay. But every new experience brings the chance to enrich my life and I plan on doing what I can to do just that, one day and one experience at a time, with friends and family there to share in those moments. I probably will still be a bit conservative (yes, some things don't change that much), but here's to enjoying what life has to offer.

The sun is up, I'm vertical, and it will be a good day.

October 8th - A.M.

October 8, 2013

Not quite sure how to describe yesterday other than it wasn't hat I had expected. Not as good as I planned, but not so bad as to be a couch potato all day. The Desert is cooling down (tomorrow is not supposed to hit 75 if you can believe that) and evening walks at sun down are a special time to enjoy the views of the surrounding mountains.

This process continues to be ever changing and learning to adjust my expectations is just another thing to deal with. For those who know me "well", yes, I really am trying to learn to be a bit more flexible. No promises, but trying.

I continue the effort to rebuild some strength for the next chemo session - which for now I prefer to ignore as it is still a week away and there are more enjoyable things to do first. Chemo is the necessary evil to rid the cancer from my body so its not a terrible experience - I just want to enjoy the more pleasant things before the next "whac a mole" session. Yes, I plan to find a "whac a mole" game at some point to exact *revenge* on the mole!

Thanks to Kim and Chuck for the picture from our walk this past Sunday morning. I managed a mile (slowly but still a mile) and then they continued for another 2. I take my victories where I find them, believe me.

The sun is up and I'm vertical - it is a good day.

October 10th A.M.

October 10, 2013

Road Trip!

I got a chance to take a trip back to the La Mirada area yesterday afternoon so Autumn could participate in her monthly Bunko game. We left with what we thought was plenty of time only to find the first rains of the Fall making a mess of the freeways. Add a truck that jack knifed across four lanes of the freeway we were on and a two-hour drive ended up taking four and a half. But it all ended well as Autumn got to her game and I got to have dinner with Arielle and Ryan at one of our favorite little Mexican hang outs. We ran into some friends as well so the chance to catch up a bit after our move was a pleasant extra.

We got back to the Desert this morning after a pretty drive with snow on the mountains surrounding the LA Area and the Desert. Its nice to have had the chance to get out for a night, and equally good to be home.

I've dealt with some nausea issues over the past week and have found that a nausea pill in the morning makes the day much more tolerable. Yeah for modern medicine.

The sun is up; I've been vertical already so it really is a good day.

October 11th - Afternoon

October 11, 2013

On a glorious day Autumn and I went and walked around the Living Desert here in Palm Springs (www.livingdesert.org). If you come to the Coachella Valley and have a little time, it is a quaint little zoo, with a wide range of animals, including giraffes, camels and big horn sheep. Better yet, it's a pleasant walk, which we did in a little over 2 1/2 hours (and with no urgency on our part). It really added to the concept of the sun being up and my being vertical.

I continue to hear from friends from across the country and believe me, it helps me as much as I know it helps many who I get to talk to. This chapter will end with me being healthy again and every reach out adds to the strength I feel in getting to that eventuality.

There's not much more to add today - it is and has been a very good day. Thanks for continuing to follow me in this journey.

October 12th

October 12, 2013

Today (or better put this morning) was spent joining hundreds of breast cancer survivors, care givers and current patients in "Paint El Paseo Pink" sponsored by the Desert Cancer Foundation (http://desertcancerfoundation.org). I learned about the event yesterday. It felt good to join in support of the efforts to cure breast cancer and while I'm dealing with non-Hodgkin lymphoma, being able to participate was up lifting.

We never know whom we touch and while I did not know anyone walking I met a breast cancer survivor (clear now for seven years) and whose daughter was just diagnosed with breast cancer. I enjoyed the morning stroll up and down El Paseo while having a conversation with someone new. I also saw my oncologist, who was honored for his almost 20 years of service to the Palm Springs/Palm Desert communities and breast cancer research and care. Again, being part of this new (cancer) community gives me a new outlet to give back and strength willing, that's what I will do.

Let me suggest to those of you kind enough to read these posts, that when you get the opportunity and are so inclined, a small gift of time, unwanted clothes, furniture or even money, goes such a long way to helping people like me and the thousands of others facing the specter of cancer, get through their days a small bit easier. Its now part of my world and I look forward to finding whatever way I can to help, even if its just joining others in this type of event.

The sun is up, I'm vertical and it has been a good day.

October 13th - Afternoon

October 13, 2013

I'll take progress anywhere I can find it and today was being able to walk a mile and a half in 35 minutes on the indoor track (still a bit warm in the afternoon - 81 at the moment) to try that outside. The last time I walked I worked hard to get through a tad over a half mile in 30 minutes. So while not at the 3 MPH or better pre cancer pace, I like the improvement. Plus, after eating what felt like three dinners in one last night (thanks Norm, Lulu and Sherry) and leftovers for lunch with still more to eat at some point, I needed to burn one or two calories.

Past that, the feeling of Fall is creeping in and I saw my first reminder of the end of Daylight Savings today. Remember it's the evening of November 2nd. Then we will see the earlier sunsets, cooler weather and hopefully a few strolls around the streets and greenbelts here near our home, and be that much closer to the end of the chemo protocols.

With that, enjoy your Sunday evening and give someone you love a hug, a smile and a smooch or two. You never know, the smile you get back just might make you day.

The sun is up, I'm vertical and its a good day.

October 14th - A.M.

October 14, 2013

Happy Columbus Day (celebration at least). After a wonderful dinner with friends last night, with plenty of laughs, its time for "Whac-A-Mole", round 3.

See everyone one the other side. Thanks for reading and your continued interest in my travails. The sun will be up soon and I'm vertical - it will be a good day.

October 15th - A.M. 208.3

October 15, 2013

Anyone who thinks this process of getting healthy is predictable is carrying a grave misunderstanding of (at least my) reality. Just when I think I know what to expect my reaction to the chemo changes. The session itself yesterday was pretty much as usual. Give me Benadryl and I sleep. I wake up when the Rituxan portion of the i.v. is done and then get the "CHOP" of the R-CHOP protocol. It's the after affects that are ever changing.

I got home late afternoon and the convoy of trucks that ran me over, while less than the first session's 20 (at least that was all I counted), was more than session 1 or 2's. I'll guess around ten or so. Some sweats, a grumpy stomach after all the anti-nausea medication and a less than fitful sleep. And this morning is my Neulasta shot.

The good news is the 3rd of the six chemo sessions is behind me (and when the attendant recovery time is complete I will be half-way through this process towards a clean bill of health). Each remains a mystery as to what lies before me and I just take things as they come. Yesterday, today and probably tomorrow remain the toughest days - that much remains the norm.

I will have my halfway CT scans in two weeks to see the progress that is being made in sending the alien life form back into outer space. Until then, its one hour at a time, one day at a time. I have no explanation for the weight gain over the past few days other than a serious carbo load on Saturday and effects of the chemo not appearing yet. I have no illusions of holding this weight in the next few days, but if I can keep the loss to a minimum, this would be a very good thing.

The sun is up, I'm vertical and it is a good day.

October 15ᵗʰ Afternoon

October 15, 2013

Here's some fun to brighten your (and my) day. The Today Show had a piece on the new biography of Jim Henson, who we all remember created the Muppets and who passed away in 1990 from pneumonia. One of my favorite Muppets has always been Cookie Monster (and what must have been the start of my cookie weakness, which those of you who me from meetings know where my first choice from any food offerings are - COOKIES! Oh, sorry, I should have said "cookies"). For a quick look at just one of Cookie Monster's thoughts about cookies, look at http://www.youtube.com/watch?v=9PnbKL3wuH4.

The book is by Brian Jay Jones and available in most formats, including Kindle readers. "He was a gentle dreamer whose genial bearded visage was recognized around the world, but most people got to know him only through the iconic characters born of his fertile imagination: Kermit the Frog, Bert and Ernie, Miss Piggy, Big Bird. The Muppets made Jim Henson a household name, but they were just part of his remarkable story."

I've downloaded the book and look forward to the smiles the story will bring from watching our children sit and watch Sesame Street and the overflowing room of Elmo's that Michelle has (and her first Elmo, which was actually Arielle's, that she still has with her today twenty plus years later).

I continue to hear from friends across the country as I go through this and it is truly heartwarming to know how much I have meant to so may people.

That's all for now as it is time for an afternoon siesta.

October 16th - P.M. 207.3

October 16, 2013

Well, as I have written before, predictability is not something that comes easily to the effects of each round of the chemotherapy. I wish I knew whether it was the chemo or the Neulasta shot, but each cycle has gifted me at least one night on little sleep and this round, it was last night. So by 3:00 a.m. I left Autumn to sleep in peace and went into my office to work on paperwork for the house and a few things for the office.

We got out of the house (another very needed thing today for me) and went to the outlet stores in Cabazon. The "crowd" was quite small and made the walking much easier than a weekend crowd or heaven forbid the Black Friday weekend crowd, which gathers well before 8:00 each morning. Some deals were found and it was good to get out in the fresh air.

The hard part of days like this are they are probably when I feel the worst and make it hardest on Autumn and friends. I know its part of the "ride" but it is the part I and no doubt most cancer patients dislike the most. It does make the good days that much sweeter and may this and each of these that may come before I finish this travail be few and very far between.

The sun came up, I am (and was) vertical and I got out to enjoy the day. It has still been a good day.

October 18th P.M.

October 18, 2013

Perspective is an interesting filter to our lives.

It is a good reminder that how bad one feels about their situation, others often face much more trying times. While I had one of my less good days this past Wednesday (no I did not try to hide it that much or that well), my day pales compares to others.

A friend lost his wife on Wednesday after a difficult three-year battle with ovarian cancer. The lady was a young 52. So when I look at my "bad" day, I know that as compared to he and his now deceased wife and his son's mother, I am a very lucky man.

I am fortunate to have friends and family pushing me to keep positive and get to the other end of this disease - which I will. I could have been much worse off. So days like today, where I was out and about for the morning, with a little work thrown in just because I could, are a blessing. The end of the chemo week means hopefully next week will be a bit easier and Autumn and I have things planned to take advantage of the "good week". Some of those I will save to "report" as they take place - a bit of fun to look forward to, with new and exciting adventures waiting. A short day trip to Ontario on Sunday to have lunch with Ryan and Arielle on their way back from Flagstaff for Arielle's "homecoming" at NAU; an exchange of

Oregano's wings for homemade spaghetti sauce - what a deal for both sides. And Autumn will get to start bowling again at the end of the week hopefully.

So all in all, no complaints.

The sun is up, I am vertical and I got to enjoy the fresh air. Not a bad day at all. Thanks for continuing to read and care.

October 21st A.M.

October 21, 2013

Once again I find that what I thought was my reality has been altered by the process of being cured and that I have zero control over it. Our road trip to Ontario yesterday was derailed by my body telling me "no way tall man". After fighting a bit of constipation, which I'm told is one side effect of the chemo (and beats the praying to the porcelain god concept most of the time), my system started to undo itself, it did it in a way that left me literally on the floor. Of course that was a result of fainting, a first in my life and my effort to either redecorate a hallway or my head (or both). All I know is I ended up on the ground, my falling cushioned somewhat by Autumn trying to keep me upright as best she could.

For those of you who giggle at the prospect of me being passed out and pretty much out of things, I for one can tell you with what I do remember that such is not the most congenial way to get through an hour or two.

Fortunately I was "out" for but a brief few seconds. It also doesn't do much for one's glasses, which are now in need of attention from a Lenscrafter's store so I can see out of them.

So needless to say, the road trip was cancelled. Thankfully, Arielle and Ryan were kind enough to check in on the Dad one their way home from their Flagstaff adventure (though I think the added leg wore Ryan out just a bit). He got his spaghetti sauce, Autumn got her wings, Arielle got her Dad hug and I kept putting my pieces back together again.

What all of this reminds me yet again, is that I am not the Captain of this ship; I am a passenger along for the ride (and what a ride it is). Every chance I get to keep the negative thoughts away I do, as days like yesterday are much harder than I ever imagined and no doubt harder on Autumn as well. Friends, positive thoughts and sharing some love and cheer (thank you to Gene and Peggy in Chicago who while dealing with their own end of life issues for a family member thought enough of me to send an Edible Arrangement to brighten our day (and which we attacked with some vigor last night too).

So I know that despite the setbacks (and yesterday was certainly one of those), the sun came up, I was (almost) vertical and with the love and support of family and friends, I continue to make it to the other side. It was a different, but good day, as will today be.

October 22 - A.M. 198.0

October 22, 2013

A little different thought for today as I reflect on the trials that we all go through whether it be the work that we do, the loss of a loved one or just the stress of each day as we encounter it. Listening to a song yesterday on the way home from getting my glasses back to usable shape (thank you Lenscrafter's), I thought sharing the chorus might help remind us all that we have many ways of sharing our love of friends and family:

> "Don't make a sound
> I'm the beat in your heart . .
> I'm the whisper in the wind
> I'm already there"

As I go through the cure of cancer, I am reminded that I am already there in many peoples' hearts and that warmth and strength is something that makes each day, as tough as some have been and likely will be still, survivable. There is an end to this and I will be cancer free. There are no acceptable alternatives and it's with that in mind I approach today, tomorrow and the rest of this journey. So yes, "I'm already there".

For the number above, yes, all the weight I gained has been shed so it's back to the building blocks (think smoothies).

The sun is up, I'm vertical and today is a good day with an exciting afternoon ahead of me, which I will report on tomorrow (there has to be some surprises now).

October 23 - A.M.

October 23, 2013

Yesterday I got the chance to share my cancer story with four ladies who have made it a part of their lives to enable cancer patients to feel warm and positive about the effects of chemo and the loss of one's hair (not that I had a lot to lose in the first place I know). I came across Debbie Green and The Turning Heads Project (www. turningheadsproject.org) through a story in the local newspaper a few weeks ago. I looked up the website and was immediately struck by the power of commitment the project has to making cancer victims feel less like a patient and more like the pre-cancer person they remembered. What was missing to me though was remembering that men go through the same emotions when facing cancer as women. Before yesterday, the ladies had shot 50 of what they call "Super Models" (and rightfully so) with only one man in the group.

I've noted before that timing is always an interesting thing in our lives and the day the article ran was the day I decided that the hair I hadn't already lost needed to be shaved off. It was a difficult day for me, not that losing my hair was going to be that hard, but the reality that I was normal, like every other cancer patient undergoing chemo, and losing my hair, was a hard thing to get comfortable with.

I reached out to Debbie to tell her just that - that men go through the same emotions as women and that I hoped that the goal of the Turning Heads Project was more encompassing than seeking women out who were in need of their emotional uplift. I was pleasantly surprised to get a response to my e-mail and from there a dialog that led to my joining the "Super Model" group yesterday. I should add that Debbie went through cancer herself in 2010, having been diagnosed with the exact form of cancer I have, Aggressive B-Cell, non-Hodgkin lymphoma, so there is recognition that she really does understand just what I am going through.

From the moment Autumn and I walked into the SJ Photography studio, Stacey (the photographer), Debbie, and Olga, a professional make-up artist with years of experience dealing with Presidents, dignitaries and other high profile people from her days in Washington, DC, made us feel special (Olga was even able to hide most of the bruises from my run in with the hallway way on Sunday). Never was I referenced to as a cancer victim or patient. The ladies were upbeat, warm, caring and most of all, having fun. The atmosphere was contagious and it was hard not to get caught up in the spirit that they brought to the shoot. They were joined by Ellen, who has come on board to help spread the word about the wonderful work the ladies do.

Three hours passed by almost too quickly. Autumn got caught up in the spirit of the afternoon and became a part of the shoot (and looked darn good if I say so myself).

When the ladies finish their work, I will have a book of the shoot with some of the better shots they took and a reminder of how special the ladies made me and Autumn feel about being a part of their mission, to make cancer patients feel alive, a vibrant part of the world we live in. Okay, yes, I still have kept my hand in my work as best I can, but this interaction added to feeling even more alive and able to be a contributor to my new world, that of having and I know in the end, beating cancer.

These ladies give their heart and soul to these photo shoots. You can feel their love and excitement from the moment you walk into the studio. They care about what they are doing and they want the "Model" to feel special, without smothering them with silly misintentions. Let me tell you, they do a wonderful job. Theirs is a true labor of love, as the Turning Heads Project is a 503(c)(3) tax-exempt organization and they spend their time and their limited resources without worrying about tomorrow. They worry about the person they are dealing with today and yesterday that was me.

The day was wonderful and their mission was successful. I felt like I was helping them open more doors to cancer patients and maybe my story and my embracing something new, and in my own way being able to give back to the people who reach out to help others, will lead to even bigger and better things for these ladies. They have been successful before joining forces to start this project and no doubt will be in other yet to be determined ventures. But yesterday I was their focus and it was wonderful. I know Debbie has at least one additional man to be part of the project. But the mission of the Turning Heads Project I think is now becoming more patient centric versus woman centric. And because I see the cancer patients every time I walk into the Comprehensive Cancer Center for my chemotherapy treatment(s), I know we are not just men, or just women. There are too many of both to go around. But we all likely feel the same emotional tugs when dealing with our cancers and my being able to be a part of these ladies work to give back, made the day a really great day.

The sun came up yesterday, I was vertical and it was a really great day. The sun is coming up now this morning, I'm upright and today too will be a good if not great day.

October 24th A.M. 200.6

October 24, 2013

As an update to yesterday's post the ladies at The Turning Heads Project have posted a few of the photos that were taken on the Project's Facebook page. Being as I'm not on Facebook, it took me a little bit to get to a platform where I could see all of the pictures but I did get there indeed. I know they certainly show Autumn as beautiful as ever; me, I get more comfortable with how I look ever day and these pictures are a reminder that in sickness and in health, I am who I am and I am proud of that.

To look at these, go to https://www.facebook.com/Theturningheadsproject and see how *"Geoff is Turning Heads"*. There will be more when the entire work is done, but these give you the flavor of how much fun the day was - for all of us, not just me. These ladies do incredible work (just look at the pictures) not only in the pictures they take but in how they make someone realize cancer is a word, an illness, not a cloud that should take away from one's life but is a part of life, an experience that when beaten, will make that which remains all the more richer.

My modeling day is done, but the spirit that these ladies brought to my day with them will live on for a long time and which I hope to be able to share with them and many others, as I continue my journey beating cancer, and beyond.

The sun is coming up and I am vertical. It is a good day.

October 26th A.M.

October 26, 2013

Another "cycle" nears completion and with it hopefully the halfway mark of the journey through the chemo (or Alien Be Gone - or some similar phrase) portion of this unexpected phase of my life. The past two weeks have been filled with a wide range of emotion, physical ups and downs and just about everything one could possibly imagine. This is not the time to look back as the lows were such that I will treat them as "negative thoughts" and escort them out of the house post haste!

As I was beginning to write this post this morning, I got an e-mail from Debbie Green to let me know The Turning Heads Project website had been updated with "my story". Many of you who have been kind enough to follow my almost daily musings will recognize much of the narrative from the post after the photo shoot. If you are new to these postings, let me suggest you take a few minutes to see the beautiful work Debbie, Stacy Jacob (the photographer) and their team of ladies do to make cancer patients feel so good about themselves while in the throes of their chemo regimes. I know their "magic" worked for me and there are more pictures now on the Project's website that show the current state of "my affairs" in the most flattering way imaginable. The beautiful lady in those pictures reveals just how much fun Autumn had as well, which made the experience all the more fulfilling. If you are so inclined, please go to http://turningheadsproject.org/geoff/#more-1038.

I know I've been touched by what Debbie, Stacy and Olga do and that spark of life will live on, like an Olympic flame, which has and will continue to inspire me to give back to the world of cancer patients, research or however I can. Certainly, it will be to help Debbie and The Turning Heads Project continue their work. Theirs is too good a mission among many other wonderful charitable endeavors for sure, but they reach people at a time of need with something few have found a way to deliver - joy, happiness, smiles and hugs - when cancer patients need them most.

Next week "Whac-A-Mole" round 4 begins, but whatever that brings (including the latest round of insurance company scan approval delays - yes, again), it can't undo that which being a part of The Turning Heads Project has done for me.

Early this Saturday morning, the sun is up, I'm vertical and its going to be a great day.

Thanks for continuing to care.

October 29th A.M. 207.7 ▓▓▓▓▓▓▓▓▓▓▓▓▓▓▓▓

October 29, 2013

The theoretical halfway point of treatment was yesterday. Hopefully a milestone that is in fact a positive sign that things are progressing well. The insurance company finally got on the same page with the doctors and I had the mid-way CT scan yesterday afternoon. I will get the "results" tomorrow when I see my oncologist and when the fourth round of chemo is administered (that sounds like such a sinister phrase).

I am not being overly optimist to be cautious but am looking forward to hearing that there has been good progress and that my goal of being back to full health by the beginning of 2014.

The feedback I've gotten from my modeling escapade has all been tremendous. I guess the concept of the face made for radio from my days as a swim meet announcer may not be quite accurate.

Otherwise, I don't have much to add today, as I get ready for tomorrow. But the sun came up this morning and I'm vertical. It's a good day.

October 31st A.M. ▓▓▓▓▓▓▓▓▓▓▓▓▓▓▓▓▓▓

October 31, 2013

Happy Halloween to all and may the excesses of Halloween candy not rain down too greatly on you.

Yesterday's chemo session was like the three before it, a long, slow day. I was the last patient to leave the treatment center as our start time was pushed to later in the morning than usual. Not that the amount of time it takes to have the chemo drugs run through the i.v. was any longer though. Thanks again to Benadryl for helping me (but unfortunately not Autumn) pass the first 3.5 hours while the Rituxan is administered - I basically nod off for almost all of that time. Later this morning is the Neulasta shot and so starts this round of Mr. Toad's Wild Ride.

We got the test results from the CT scan that was performed on Monday and its nice to say - Good News. The scan shows that my large (or bulky as the doctors like to say) tumor has shrunk by just over 50%. There are signs of further necrosis at the back of the tumor (also a good thing). My oncologist is very pleased and if he is pleased, then so are we. He has decided to move my remaining chemo treatments to once every three weeks from the previously set, and in his words very aggressive, every two weeks. This will give me an extra week to regain some strength before the next "Whac-A-Mole" session. I'll take each extra day and use it to my advantage. The push back (which includes moving chemo from Mondays to Wednesdays) impacts some of the upcoming personal schedule Autumn and I had tentatively lined up but we will manage. Having learned to put my health and getting better first in priority, this is just another thing to put first and that's what we will do. There remains the possibility of post chemo radiation, but that is a decision for after the December 9th PET scan. All in all, a great start to the second half of getting rid of the cancer and returning to good health.

I want to take a moment to again thank everyone who takes the time to read these musings, as well as everyone who in their own way reach out to me and Autumn to let us know they continue to follow my progress (yes, as noted above, there really is progress). Last night I received a video clip of a gathering of friends in Atlanta who were kind enough to send get well soon wishes. It made my inability to join them for this year's National Conference of Bankruptcy Judges a bit easier to take. Thanks to Ted and Amy Gavin for finding a way for me to share in their dinner and the camaraderie of friends. And for all the die-hard Boston Red Sox fans, the long night was no doubt worth the victory and the celebration - enjoy.

I continue to get wonderful feedback from my modeling. The "keep my head bald" look is leading in the vote versus letting my hair grow back post chemo. We shall see later where that ends up.

The sun is rising and I've been vertical this morning for a while (another night after chemo round of almost, but not quite insomnia; this too passes). It will be a good day.

November 2nd - P.M.

November 2, 2013

Yesterday was an interesting day. Yes, I was able to be vertical and the sun came up so it was a good day. But it was a day filled with emotions and generally left me a bit low on the energy and emotion scales.

Part of it was the knowledge of the second day after chemo, which has generally been a harder day than most for me, was again upon me. And no matter what I thought of for inspiration, I was just a bit low in the emotion tank. This does happen to us all with or without undergoing chemo.

I also knew that there was a host of activities associated with this year's National Conference of Bankruptcy Judges in Atlanta, where I would have liked to have been to be able to be with friends and colleagues. Between the ABI luncheon where Judge Barry Russell was honored as this year's recipient of the Judge William L. Norton,

Jr. Award for Judicial Excellence, the ABI Reform Commission field hearing and the installation of Judge Eugene Wedoff as the incoming President of the Conference, there was much going on I wasn't able to part take in first hand. Missing this year's conference was a disappointment.

But the day dawns anew and this morning Autumn and I went into Palm Springs for the morning. We got to meet Molly and Will of Will Stiles who lent me a couple of the shirts for my "modeling" session and they, like the Turning Heads Project ladies were, truly lovely people and so kind to share with the Turning Heads Project mission (yes, I did get one of the shirts and a dress for Autumn too).

Then we went and walked to opening day of the Palm Springs Street Fair, with lots of yummy treats (think home made tamales - some came home yes, beef jerky, fresh pastries, cookies, honeys (lemon, cinnamon, etc.) Parmesan crisps in varying flavors, fresh gyro sandwiches, and lots of artists. On a glorious 80+ degree late morning, the walk was fun and filled with good tastes. I even got to have an old fashion macaroon cookie.

A few more stops on the way home and the day has been a thousand percent more uplifting than yesterday - it helped that I'm feeling a bit better too, though still tired from the chemo.

But before the clocks fall back tonight and Standard Time returns, the sun has been up and I've been out to enjoy it. It is a good day.

November 5th A.M.

November 5, 2013

Early morning post the end of daylight savings and I think while I have adjusted, finally the cats may have succumbed to the change and are now letting me sleep again until 5:00 a.m. (so kind of them isn't it). More seriously, what is apparent to me is the aggressive schedule of chemo I've been on has in fact taken a bit more of a toll on me than I had imagined. I now have a better appreciation for the pace of the chemo and just how tired I truly have been while dealing with the once every two-week protocol. Powering through was what I did because that is what I know and now I need and will take advantage of the extra week to rest.

Today marks the end of the first (or what I had been calling the "bad" week) post chemo. Yesterday was the first day I started to gain a bit of strength - though at the end of the afternoon. The latest change is when I have a decent size meal I tend to almost immediately fall into a hard sleep. I don't think I can call it a nap, as it is a pretty deep snooze. I guess my body concentrates at one thing at a time right now. Oh well, so be it.

Autumn has had a chance to restart her bowling activities subbing in the Fun City Strikers (yes a senior league for Sun City residents). I got to watch her yesterday and seeing her back in the bowling world brings a smile to both of us. The fact that she is better than almost everyone in the league doesn't hurt either and the ladies on the team she is subbing on are enjoying her company and she theirs. That makes me feel good too. As for me, I'm not pressing the bowling concept yet as I doubt seriously that I have the strength to bowl without threatening to fall face first (or otherwise) onto the lanes. Just another something to look forward to when good health is restored.

Autumn and I continue to look for ways to help the ladies at the Turning Heads Project and are getting them some pro bono assistance so they can take their gifts more nationwide. I keep hearing stories of how they have been approached to help people feel so much better about their status as a cancer patient, including one last night where a lady in hospice care wanted to be a model. Arrangements were made and while wheelchair bound, the lady got to experience the joy that the Project brings. Efforts are underway to get her her "book" of pictures before she loses her fight. But the chance to feel that special for a few hours, into the throes of her cancer fight, surely made the lady, and I have no doubt, the Turning Heads Project ladies, feel good. It is rewarding to be able to be a part of their mission.

Routines are now settling in and the cool weather brings the snow birds back to the Desert, with a bit more increased pace to daily activities. I continue to work towards good health, trying to leave my frustrations about inabilities at the front gate to our house.

But the sun is up, I'm vertical and today, like yesterday, is a good day.

November 6th A.M.

November 6, 2013

So I find myself again looking back at the post chemo week utterly amazed that there is no predictability to how I get through each day. What I do know is that the efforts to have a routine for each day are all but a wasted effort.

Yesterday started out well but by the end of the day I was feeling pretty blah (yes a medical term for crappy). Seems that the last couple of post chemo weeks have gone this way where about the time

I thought I would feel good I feel much worse than I expected (or hoped). Followed by a long night of interrupted sleep, I am not sure if I am the windshield or the bug - or both (probably both).

Each day brings its own challenges but the physicality of dealing with the effects of chemo, besides the effect on the tumor, do leave me occasionally weak in the knees (figuratively if not literally). And so I count my blessing that yesterday is behind me, today has new challenges and hopes, and tomorrow is hopefully one day closer to putting cancer behind me.

I continue to marvel at just how people can get through this without the type of love and support I have been so fortunate to have. Their must be an inner strength that rivals anyone anywhere. All I can say is the next time you see someone dealing with cancer, please be a bit less afraid to give them encouragement, support or how ever you feel so inclined. It makes a huge difference to us and I bet you will feel good too.

The sun is now up, I'm vertical and while yesterday turned out to be a less good (or okay) day than I would have hoped, today will be a good day. Thanks for continuing to read these musings from my side of cancer.

November 8th A.M. 202.4

November 8, 2013

I wish I could come up with something pithy, or wonderfully insightful to share this morning but that's just not the space I'm in today. Instead, its another day of working to get some strength back, gain a couple of pounds (yes, I really am just above 200 yet again) and hoping to get a regular sleep pattern back.

Figuring I don't have much control over any of the above, I will just focus on making today a better than good day and how best to utilize the extra week between chemo treatments. We have some work being completed around the house next Monday and Friday (finally) and then our family room will be complete, with the entertainment center and sound system installed. We have dinner with the ladies from the Turning Heads Project as well, (as well as their husbands too) and we look forward to sharing an evening of warmth and joy with them. Besides that, it is day by day, in the dog days of getting through this process.

May today bring each of you who read this a ray of sunshine, a moment or two of peace and comfort and the chance to reflect of how you can fill your lives with something up-beat and positive. No doubt a family outing, a hug or two and just the chance to enjoy friends and family will make the weekend that much brighter, and remember that while I continue my journey, it will end on a positive note with a clean bill of health - there is for me no other alternative that I will accept.

The sun is up, I'm vertical and it is a good day.

November 11th A.M.

November 11, 2013

A hearty welcome to a new week and for many, an extended weekend. For me, it's been a few days of still feeling the effects of the last chemo session. This is the most extended timeframe post-chemo that

I have felt less than "chipper" and seems that the cumulative nature of the treatments has been catching up with me. The new phrase around the house is "Charming" and no doubt I have been living up to it. Sometimes no matter how hard one tries (almost too hard it seems) the reality of the task I've faced comes down and coupled with a persistent dry cough (purportedly allergy related, from what I don't know or have a clue), I just have a hard time staying upbeat. I am glad to have an extra (dare I say "normal") third week to try to feel a bit better. I'm sure Autumn could use the feeling better time on my part too.

We got to take a short road trip Saturday afternoon to Buena Park yesterday to celebrate Autumn's upcoming birthday, especially as, happy birthday to her, my next chemo session falls on her actual birthday. Probably less fun for me than her but still . . . . so we went in to share an afternoon with Ryan and Arielle and dinner at the Rain Forest Cafe at Downtown Disney along with our friends Kim and Chuck. Dinner was fun (though the food got mixed reviews from the group, mine not counting as taste remains a moving target sometimes on a meal to meal basis). Dessert was beignets, almost as good as the New Orleans originals, from the Jazz Kitchen in Downtown Disney. I promise, the almost like Dumont's didn't stop our group, as many of the acquired delights did not make it to the car and the return to the Whitacre's abode.

The week ahead holds interesting promise, with hopefully the installation of the wall unit we planned when we moved in and the sound system that has been waiting in the wings pending the wall unit. Dinner with some friends and another bowling league for Autumn to partake in while one of the people we met recovers from surgery to repair a broken kneecap suffered while walking his dogs and missing a curb. So Autumn's non-care-giving routine is starting to fill in as if I were working a bit more full time and as we thought, neither of us will suffer from inactivity for too long.

A shout out back to the Tan Man, who continues to marvel us with his spirit as he undergoes his surgeries and rehabilitation from his heart value issues. Here is a portion of his most recent post:

"This Thursday the 14th I am going back into the hospital for another cardiac cath. Dr. Goldstein is going to put a stent in my left pulmonary artery because my aorta is pressing on it. Hopefully, this will be all I'll need until that last surgery (the Fontan) when I am 3 or 4."

Hard to complain about a few rounds of chemo at age 60 when this little guy is barely six months old, has been through multiple surgeries with more to go. It's a reminder that no matter how bad we think things are for us, there are always people facing much worse trials and tribulations in their lives. So yes Mr. Tan Man, we will both get past our respective hurdles and hugs will get shared sooner than either of us can imagine. Keep setting an example we all can be proud of (and that goes to mom, dad and grandma too as you are all part of this process).

The most recent picture added to the gallery is from my Turning Heads Project shoot. Amazing what a talented artist can do with a tired old(er) guy.

So with that as a backdrop, the sun is rising and I'm vertical. It is a good day. Enjoy it to your fullest, whatever that may be. Thanks for continuing to read and care.

November 13th A.M.

November 13, 2013

Autumn and I got to spend a wonderful evening with Debbie, Stacy, Olga (and their husbands) and Ellen from the Turning Heads Project last night as we celebrated the special way they bring joy to people's lives (and we broke in our home with its first dinner party). As with the photo shoot, we had a great time, with lots of laughter, stories and just how many ways these ladies touch people.

I got my book from the photo shoot as well and more than just pictures, it's filled with inspiration to remind those of us going through chemotherapy that there is another side to our journey, which I know for me will be a clean bill of health. There are no favorites within these quotes and many that stood out.

My limo certainly hit a large pothole and/or broke down. Autumn is on that bus besides me. The picture on the page with the quote about riding the bus is of me and Autumn looking beautiful and both of us content. Very fitting indeed. And thanks to all of you reading these posts for joining me on my bus as I deal with this phase of life.

Beyond that, the sun has risen, I'm vertical and today is the beginning of the first extra week in-between chemo sessions. It is a very good day.

November 14th A.M.

November 14, 2013

One rightfully can describe the trial of cancer in that it did sneak up on me. But I bought a big bat and with the help of a wonderful team of doctors and nurses, friends, family and supporters, this cancer picked the wrong person. I'm not afraid to swing my bat and as I've shared, that bat has been achieving great results so far.

I've written throughout this journey about the power of being positive and whether it has been 1%, 50% or 99.9% of the reasons for my success to date (aside from modern medicine), it does make a difference. So when faced with something unforeseen and less enthralling than you might have hoped, grab your bat and swing with a big smile on your face - it makes a huge difference.

If you would like a brief interlude in your day with more pictures from my photo shoot day with the Turning Heads Project ladies, please click on the following link: http://vimeo.com/78728839. The fun Autumn and I had is evident in these pictures (even the one we lovingly call my "Uncle Fester" look (for you younger folk, that is a reference to the original Adams Family show - go look it up and like the Road Runner/Wiley E. Coyote), smile, laugh and enjoy.

The sun is coming up, I'm vertical and it is a good day.

November 17th P.M. ▓▓▓▓▓▓▓▓▓▓▓▓▓▓▓

November 17, 2013

Week three between chemo treatments has felt a great deal like the prior week two's - some recovery but not near anything that I expected (oh darn, there is that expectation thing again). Still moving slowly but moving nonetheless.

Today we picked up two free Thanksgiving turkeys so we will be well stocked for turkey meat round the house. A lunch of fish tacos that rival Rubio's and then back to the homestead.

I got to get out on a golf course today! No silly folks, not a regulation course as there is no way I can navigate one of those and stay upright as my "resting" pulse rate remains well north of 100. Nope, Autumn and I played the Sun City 18 hole putting course, which just reopened after its Fall over seeding. While open, the grass hasn't been mowed down to green shortness, so it was like putting through molasses, or a long-haired Siamese cat's fur. But we had a good time and enjoyed the 90 minutes in the sunshine. I even had two holes in ones (a miracle believe me). Some of the same old bad habits haven't been affected by the chemo (phooey) but I started to figure out the fix near the end.

The coming week is filled with things for the house, Autumn's bowling (3) leagues and "whac-a-mole" round 5. There is also Autumn's birthday on Tuesday for good measure.

I was pleased to hear how well the Tan Man did with his latest procedure. As for weight gain measures my friend, tell mom, dad and grandma you want a smoothie or two. That will help with the weight gain for sure!

For everyone dealing with things more catastrophic than me, know that our hearts are with you in support; if you are having a "bad day", someone beyond you likely is having one that is worse.

But the sun has been shining, I'm upright, and it has been a good day.

November 19th A.M.

November 19, 2013

The migration south of the snow-birds appears to be well underway as the activity level in our community, as well as in the greater Palm Springs/Palm Desert/Rancho Mirage/La Quinta communities has been significantly increasing over the past week to ten days. It serves to remind me that many of those who call the Desert their home for the winter bring with them issues far greater than mine and that each day for me hopefully brings me one day closer to being cancer free.

It is also a time for a bit of reflection, something that I seem to get a bit more time to do than I might have imagined. Ours is a very good life, with a grand child on the way, children comfortable in their respective surroundings, our new home where we are starting to get more comfortable by the day with new neighbors and friends I look at what I bring to these facets of life, along with my work environment, and feel that while I no doubt could (and hopefully will) do more, I and we are doing well and contributing more than we take from our daily lives.

Today is likely a function for me of tomorrow, another round of chemo and one step closer to being through this months long escapade. It still boggles the mind to think people have to try to do this alone and I for one don't know how they manage. Its been difficult enough for me to get through with my support groups - it just means one should be even more in awe of those who in fact survive, become cancer free and are able to give back yet again, despite the hardships they face. Each of my issues, from whatever world, pale to what so many others face.

So I turn to today, with workmen getting things installed around the house (finally), importing some music for future listening pleasure and just knowing that the sun is up, I'm vertical and it's a good day.

May yours be good as well.

November 20th A.M.

November 20, 2013

The world famous philosopher *"Snoopy"*, when asked by Peppermint Patty what can you do when you're having a bad week and everything seems hopeless, replied with a "SMAK (kiss)!! The point being *"A little bit of love makes all the difference"*.

Remember that not everyone is having a good or great day, but a little bit of kindness, tenderness and love will not only make someone else feel better, it will make you feel better. With thanks to our friend Lisa who brought that reminder to Autumn and me yesterday.

As for today, the sun will be up soon, I'm vertical and while today is whac-a-mole round 5, it will be a good day.

November 21st A.M.

November 21, 2013

Chemo round 5 is now behind me with the Neulasta shot to complete the protocol later this morning. Then I'm down to the last (scheduled) round which will be on December 11th all things remaining as they are. After that there is a possibility (no I will not predict any percentage probability) of radiation to finalize the Alien Be Gone process. That decision is in Dr. Camacho's hands and will be dependent on the PET scan being done on December 9th.

For now, its recuperation time from this fifth round and with another "extra" week to get some strength back, the goal (per the doctor) is to get closer to my pre cancer strength from last July versus the current state of feeling run over by a steam roller (for a better description, go back to one of my earlier posts re the Road Runner and Wiley E. Coyote; the steam roller is a bit more potent than Acme Manufacturing's version and my pieces take a tad bit longer to reassemble). We would like that return to have already happened. Okay, but now five rounds of chemo in, my expectations are a tad bit lower - not much, how about by December 9th or Christmas Day and quoting Alvin and the Chipmunks, "We can hardly stand to wait, so Christmas don't be late").

I plan on continuing the here-to-for process of getting out of the house every day to do something, be it a walk at the clubhouse or around our block, walking the mall (though post Thanksgiving that will press the "no mall during the Holidays rule), using the 18 hole putting course, going to a movie or just a meal out. Last night Autumn and I joined some of the people we have met here in our community for a round or two of bocce ball. I even joined in and a good time, with lots of laughs and good-natured ribbing was enjoyed by all. It's nice to be included by a number of our neighbors so quickly. And as I frankly expected, my cancer is a non-issue with so many people here; it's almost expected that health issues affect us all at some time as we grow older and its just my turn in the barrel. So being a bit accommodating (*i.e.* a chair by the court so I wasn't standing all night) was no big issue. In fact everyone wanted to make sure I was enjoying the evening and participating as best I could - no sympathy, just glad to see me out especially after the 5.5 hour chemo session.

Our entertainment center and sound system are FINALLY installed (yeah!). A bit of touch up and that phase will be complete. A bit of work to finish the remodel of our guest bathroom and a few other handyman assists and we will be ready for Thanksgiving. Whether my appetite joins the festivities is a TBD.

Thanks for continuing to read as I move through this journey. With that, the sun will be rising soon (yes, another post chemo light sleep evening aided by a pestering cat at 3:00 this morning) and I'm vertical. It will be a good day.

November 22nd A.M.

November 21, 2013

The Neulasta shot effects finally hit me late yesterday afternoon, slowing my day down to a slow melt into the couch. I got a lot done before the slowdown so the day was not a total loss by any means. Its good to be getting the effects behind me so the rebuilding of strength can begin in earnest soon.

As we move into the Holiday Season, for those of you looking for another way to give to those of us fighting cancer, please look at "Cycle for Survival". It's a charity raising money for Memorial Sloan Kettering's rare cancer research program, including research into lymphomas like my non-Hodgkin type (and one of the facilities a friend offered to get me into if I wasn't getting the kind of care I have in fact been getting from Desert Regional Medical Center's Comprehensive Cancer Center in Palm Springs). Jennifer and David Linn of Oak Point Partners started it when Jennifer was diagnosed with a rare cancer. Suggested by Ted and Amy Gavin, each year they and their "team" ride for their friends and loved ones who have fought or are fighting cancer. This year, Amy and Ted are riding for Amy's mom and for me - for which I am very touched. Amy and Ted have put out a challenge to their team that they are matching everything their team raises. Here's the link to their team page: http://mskcc.convio.net/site/TR/CycleforSurvival/AG Cycle Event?team_id=34 033&pg=team&fr_id=2090

Every dollar people give to places like Cycle for Survival, or the Turning Heads Project which took my "Super Model" photos that I have talked about before, or the Desert Research Foundation which raises money to help those who can't afford the cost of their treatments, Guilda's Club, or any of the hundreds of other wonderful organizations across the country, helps support people like me, who never imagined they would be a cancer patient and for me, hopefully soon, a cancer survivor, as well as the research to reduce and one day end the ravishes of cancer. Mine is not a plea for money but rather a reminder that if I can fall victim to cancer, so can many others we know. It has made me feel good to help others through my journey and sharing that goodness is much easier for me today than before I became a cancer patient.

Many I have talked to through my journey tell me of their contributions in my name - I am truly honored to be so well thought of. I have made it a point to share in my expectation of beating my cancer by making contributions to a number of cancer organizations this year and I hope each of you, in your own way, find sharing in your good health, so others not so fortunate can share as well.

The sun is rising, I'm vertical and today, like the days before and the days to come, will be a good day.

November 23rd P.M. 205.7

November 23, 2013

Its been a good day, despite being only a couple of days since chemo round five. Autumn and I played "Couples Putters" with our friends Norm and Lulu on the 18 hole putting course, on a beautiful morning, with good friends and had a lot of fun. Autumn of course had the "best" shot of the day covering for one of my less than stellar "tee shots" (alternate shot format) not that that should surprise anyone. Followed by lunch at Boulevards and seeing other friends coming through the restaurant made for a wonderful morning.

Of course this close to chemo that level of exercise followed by food (in my case, a slice of mud pie as everything except maybe ice cream tastes like a load of salt has been poured on it), meant a nice snooze on the couch when we got home. But I was able to get out and enjoy friends, fresh air and feeling alive.

I need to correct a reference to a local charity here in the Desert from a prior post. The correct charity is the Desert Cancer Foundation (www.desertcancerfoundation.org) rather than the Desert Research Foundation. Sorry for any confusion.

The DSI Holiday Party is going on tonight in Chicago and this year, I'm there in spirit. The fact that I'm missing 20 degree weather is a plus, but this close to chemo there would have been no way to manage the travel, the party and the return.

Next up of course is Thanksgiving Week and Arielle comes out tomorrow, with Ryan on Wednesday and friends arriving on Tuesday. It will be good to have family and friends to help celebrate that which I, and all of us, have to be thankful for. None the least of which is my getting better and I hope a relatively soon return to clean, non-cancer, health.

With that, as the sun gets ready to set, I can say the sun rose this morning, I was vertical and able to enjoy the fresh air. It's been a good day.

November 27th A.M.

November 27, 2013

As we head into the Thanksgiving Holiday, I for one have much to be thankful for as no doubt everyone reading this does. First, I am thankful for the doctors who initially would not accept the status quo and continued to look to find that which proved to be my cancer and then diagnosed the heck out of me to determine exactly what it was and how to treat it. Then to those here at the Comprehensive Cancer Center for their caring in my treatment. I look forward to saying "good bye for now" hopefully in the coming weeks.

To my friends, from all facets of my life, who have reached out, either by Guestbook comments, private e- mails, telephone calls or letters, to let me know I was in their thoughts, prayers etc. Hugs of course as well. Everyone who has reached out has made a difference in how I have made it through so far. I can't ever fully express my gratitude for the caring other than I'm still here and not going anywhere anytime soon if I can help it.

To my colleagues, both at DSI and in the ABI, who have made my absence a bit easier to swallow both personally and professionally. The absence, from my point of view is not easy nor how I would have wanted to carry out my responsibilities.

To those around me here in the Desert whom Autumn and I have met, new friends, who have accepted me and my cancer as more of a matter of life than a penalty brought down upon me. To the angels from the Turning Heads Project and many others, yours has been a gift of kindness and joy that fills one's heart with the strength to carry on each day, even when those days are a bit less than we might have hoped for (yes, the last couple of days were that way and ergo the reason for the radio silence).

To Autumn, Arielle, Ryan, Michelle, my mom and sister, who never expected me to be the first to have to deal with such unnerving news as to our health, but who have weathered this storm so much better than one could ever hope for. Their strengths, in their own way, give me the strength to face each new day, each new hurdle, with as much fervor and an attitude of success. I have much to live for and be thankful for.

As the Holiday comes into full swing, let me add thanks to friends who have come to share in our celebration and Allan and Sharon, your presence means a great deal to this special celebration. May each of you revel in the joys of today, the kindness of friends and family, the miracle of life and medicine (Tan Man, watch how much turkey you eat please) and the knowledge that

The sun has risen, we are vertical and it is a great day!

December 1, 2013 A.M.

December 1, 2013

Thanksgiving has come and now fades into memories of times spent with family and friends, all good and refreshing one's spirit to face anew the remaining task before me. My down days have memories of laughter and cheers to beat back the negative thoughts that still try to creep into my consciousness. Thanks to Allan and Sharon, Arielle and Ryan, and of course Autumn, for being here to make the memories such enjoyable ones.

I'm still facing maybe the hardest days of the chemo treatment cycle as I have found that the rumor that chemo has a cumulative effect on those of us "lucky" enough to deal with this cure is true.

My mornings seem pretty decent, my afternoons fall into a bit of lethargy and evenings are a complete hit and miss (mostly miss so far this cycle). Food remains an iffy subject and choices for dinner seem to be getting less and less. Make no mistake about it, I still eat, drink (smoothies) and work on the "be merry" part. I have another week of recuperation before the next and last cycle begins so there will be plenty of trying to feel better to be undertaken. I'm not going to try to get to Los Angeles for the ABI program, as while it means a great deal to me to be there, getting past my cancer is more important than one or two meetings and a chance to see friends from across the country. I will get to see the friends next year, count on it and there will be more meetings.

I got to try our putting course a couple of times this past week, including yesterday with Ryan. He got a hole in one - I managed to come close to his score and a good time was had by both of us. There is a bunny rabbit that calls the course home and that led me to thinking of the classic Bugs Bunny cartoon "What's Opera Doc?" For some of you who haven't experienced the joys of this classic cartoon, try http://vimeo.com/105781176 and give up seven minutes of your day. I hope your smile will make the time more than worth it. I have been known to chime in with *"Kill the Wabbit"* on many an occasion though of course I would never do that in real life. For our putting course bunny, just leave the ball where it lies please.

The sun is up and I am vertical. Today, like the most recent days including the Holiday, have been good days. May yours be as well.

December 2nd A.M.

December 2, 2013

Least one think that this journey has no emotional swings, let me tell you that is just not the case. No matter how much we think we are or have vented emotions, they boil to the surface when one least expects. Even for me, despite what I think are really good efforts, emotions run high and spill into frustration that colors judgment and impacts family and friends.

I haven't ever claimed to be perfect and this process highlights my (and likely most patients) imperfections. Try as I might, the frustrations of being so dependent on others for almost everything become flash points of emotion that when erupting, can cause harm to others and ourselves. I wouldn't suggest bottling one's emotions inside themselves, for that is as negative a concept as allowing the downward or depressing thoughts to color our efforts to recover. Venting every little frustration is equally as negative and destructive. All it does is leave one sorry for hurting those who mean well and are trying to help. Where the middle ground is obviously a personal matter and try as I might, it remains a moving target and each day's target is not necessarily the same as yesterday's, today's or even tomorrow's.

The reality is we are frail, with needs that just can't always be met. A bigger truth is I am frail in many ways, with needs that can't always be met and try as I may, I fail. The good news is failure is a trait of the living and that, by all means, remains my number one priority. I expect to beat this cancer in the coming weeks and then focus my resolve to regaining my strength and returning to a routine a bit more along the lines of what I envisioned when we moved to the Desert. (Note the emphasis on "a bit more" as no doubt the life lesson from this escapade is one need not kill themselves working to then miss out on enjoying life!).

The sun is up (the subterranean termites are meeting their demise at the expense of our pocket book and sanity as the pest control company drills holes around our house to get rid of them with whatever they use as I sit here typing) and I am vertical. It is and will be a good day.

December 4th A.M. 208.1

December 4, 2013

We decided a small display of holiday spirit was appropriate in the house and yesterday added a small tree to our family room to help brighten things up a bit. Little did we know that the "girls" had to approve of our choice of trees. By the attached I think you will note that they in fact "approved". At least they did not want to climb the tree - even a 3 1/2 footer would have been problematic.

Today marks the start of the second third extra week and I will admit to feeling a bit better than in the past. However, that feeling tends to be fleeting and mid to late afternoons and evenings remain a vestige of naps, tired legs and little energy to move to the rest of any given daily activity. Not that this stops me, but it does slow me down (anyone catch the last 30 minutes of the Voice last night? - no worries, I know the results). So a bit of rest after a visit from friends in for the ABI Winter Leadership Conference in Rancho Palos Verdes (thanks Ted and Amy) and then off to Bocci in the evening.

News as to progress will come next week - sorry, no previews, as I truly don't have anything more to report and won't until after the December 9th PET scan.

The sun is up, I'm vertical and it is a good day.

December 6th A.M.

December 6, 2013

Welcome to sunny and frigid Southern California. For those of you from parts back East, this may seem tame but for this native Southern Californian, it is just COLD! Okay, blah blah and all that stuff.

I'm working through my second week three between chemo treatments and finding that during the day I seem to be feeling better (for the most part). So of course, I try to stay up a bit later and wham, I don't wake up until well past my normal wake up hour. That needless to say aggravates the felines in the house, as they don't get fed when they want. Oh well, they will survive somehow. (Yes, they have been fed this morning or I could not be sitting here typing this entry.) And so like everything that has transpired before now, I have NO clue what to expect today, tomorrow or next week, *except* on the 11th, when the sixth round of chemo is administered - then we work through that cycle.

The COLD is also a reminder of other things we deal with through our lives. I'm reminded that mine, while trying and at times a serious downer, can pale to the trials and tribulations others may be going through.

Marriages that fall apart for reasons beyond our comprehension, which at the Holidays only seem that much harder to deal with, or the declining health of a parent, the loss of a loved one, all make mine easier to deal with because I will beat this - and come out the other side ready for the next round of life's adventures.

Take a moment to look around you and count your blessings (a form of thinking positive I know but still) versus the difficulties and stresses. You might find the ray of sunshine easier to look at versus the storm clouds of dismay and despair. Then take that smile and share it with someone who needs it - even a hug makes a difference (don't I know and understand that). Call it a form of spreading Holiday cheer. Pass it forward - a form of pay it forward as the saying goes. You'll feel better (I already do this morning) and I bet the recipient(s) will too.

Finally this morning, a shout out for multiple birthday greetings to my father-in-law Bill, my son-in-law Ryan, and good friend Paul. They all share today as their birthday - a blessing to all who know them and get the chance to share a bit of our lives with them. So HAPPY BIRTHDAY!

The sun is up, I'm vertical (its still COLD) - it is a good day.

December 7th A.M.

December 7, 2013

Another chilly morning but that is hardly news anywhere around the country, let alone here in the Desert. Yesterday brought a try at some more strenuous physical activity in honor of week three - but with less than hoped for results.

I took out the bowling ball while Autumn was bowling her Friday morning league. What I learned quickly was that I don't have the strength in my legs that I need for that level of activity. Sure, walking is easier than right after chemo, but planting my leg and controlling the slide while releasing the bowling ball was all but non- existent. Very disappointing. So while trying was a good sign, the lack of strength was almost depressing. Add a high pulse rate after only a few tries and it didn't take a rocket scientist to know, I'm not ready.

I want to be further along than this, but my wants don't equal reality. Another failure for Type A's in this process - we don't control a darn thing!

So its back to making sure I take small, more controlled steps as I prepare for the next round of chemo and the process of regaining my health. There are no magic wands, no special elixirs or pills, just time, hard work and patience that it will all be fine in the end.

I did miss seeing friends at the ABI Winter Leadership Conference these past couple of days in Rancho Palos Verdes and have heard from many that I was missed. Its nice to be remembered while I go through this but missing the in-person contact is also hard. And to bring things even more fully into light, I read an article this morning in this week's Sports Illustrated (yes, the print version still exists somehow) about one of the children lost in the Newton, CT Sandy

Hook Elementary School shooting titled "What We Lost". The story is a reminder that every life is precious and those taken away, for whatever reason, impact us in ways we can't always imagine let alone comprehend.

Mine is a life being saved, through the work of talented doctors and the support of friends and loved ones. It is a life to be shared, enjoyed and cherished. That is my goal today, tomorrow and each day in my future.

So with the sun now up and being vertical, it is a good day. I hope yours is as well.

December 9th A.M.

December 9, 2013

A fun day in the "warm" sunshine yesterday as we went to the Annual Tamale Festival in nearby Indio. For those of you who enjoy true homemade tamales, the range of tastes was outstanding. Granted, there were a few flavors that were not anywhere near what I would choose (blueberry tamales - no thanks), but to each their own. Autumn and I ended up with a bag filled with great flavors, for consumption over the next couple of days or later, assuming a few make the freezer.

The yearly zucchini bread bake was completed last night with the better part of forty loaves made. We got smart this year (no comment please) and used aluminum foil baking pans, so no cleaning the pans after each use; we just left them in their respective pans and will give the loaves out to their recipients pans and all. Much easier on the baker and her cleaning assistant.

Today is supposed to be my pre-final chemo PET scan. Of course, I'm waiting for the insurance company and the doctor's office to agree that the scan is a necessary part of the treatment regimen so I may not stray far from the house so I can go on short notice if need be. Aren't insurance companies great to have as friends? Oh well, we all know they are in business to make money, not spend it. And so it goes - this too will pass.

The reminders of our good fortune, even while dealing with cancer, are too plentiful for me to ignore. Autumn read an article today about homebound seniors without families or friends who can use basic necessities this Holiday season. No, not toys or gifts, but things like soap, toilet paper, postage stamps. Then there are the food drives for those who may not get a decent meal over the Holidays. It is a harsh reminder that so many people live at or near the poverty level, even here is what people think is the well to do Palm Springs and surroundings. Sure, the rich and famous have made the Palm Springs area home for decades and things like the former Bob Hope Chrysler Classic (now the Humana - Clinton Global Initiative Golf Classic), the work done by Sonny Bono when he was mayor to bring the arts back to the area all make this seem like an enclave of well to do people. But there is a large migrant worker community in the Coachella Valley (as well of course in other large farm rich environs) as well as an aging population, many of whom are all alone. One person told the article's author that except for the daily delivery from the Meals on Wheels driver who delivers his meals and the occasional check up from neighbors, he has almost no daily contact with others.

We often walk past collection boxes for food drives, or the Salvation Army bell ringers without giving them much of a thought. This year, having gone through the last five months of my fight with cancer, has made both of us more aware of how lucky we are despite my cancer. Giving a few cans of food to a food drive, or a package of paper towels or toilet paper, shouldn't be a big thing and this year, is something we are happily doing. We won't miss those cans of food or paper goods and we are helping those who can use a helping hand.

So as I start this week and the hopefully final chemo treatment (radiation is still TBD) I give thanks for what I have in my life and that by sharing a few things with others, the spirit of Christmas can burn brighter for those much less fortunate. The sun is up, I'm vertical and with giving a bit, it's a good day.

December 11ᵗʰ A.M.

December 11, 2013

Today' post will be short. Yes, it is still *chilly* around here so wherever you may be, I feel your cold too. The PET scan remains an issue between the doctors and the insurance carrier (something about not authorizing more than one every six months - okay, whatever, just resolve it).

Before heading off to "Whac-A-Mole" round six and hopefully final, let me leave you with this. It has been twenty years since Jim Valvano made his impassioned speech at the inaugural ESPY Awards. If you haven't seen this five minute speech, or its been a while, take a look at this link http://www.youtube.com/watch?v=PNKJNNbPCEc. What you will find is a road map to addressing and surviving cancer or whatever peril blocks your path in life. He of course could not survive his cancer and by the time of the speech he was near his death. But the motivation and inspiration continues with now over $100 million raised for cancer research. More importantly his words live on for all of us -

"Don't give up, don't ever give up."

The sun is up, I'm vertical, and it will be a good day.

December 11th P.M.

December 11, 2013

Welcome to the world of insurance. After talking with the "representative" (I prefer dingbat but that might be giving them too much credit), I learn that purportedly the carrier has been trying to reach me. First they claim to have left messages at our old landline (how they can do that with a disconnected number is beyond me); then they claimed to have left messages on my cell phone - really? As if that number is ignored for days on end.

The result is the PET scan got approved this morning and will now be conducted on Friday. Then the doctor "postponed" today's chemo so he could see the results of the PET scan. And so after a couple of hours, no chemo today; no news today and there should be something to report come Friday or early next week. And the "R" word was mentioned again, so that remains a possibility.

We did get clarification on the original size of my tumor. When Autumn asked the doctor he told her BIGGER than a softball. Of course I don't do much that is quiet or small so why should the tumor be anything different.

The sun is still up (and its in the mid 60's); I'm still upright and it is a good day.

December 14, 2013 A.M. ▨▨▨▨▨▨▨▨

December 14, 2013

The results of the PET scan are in and the news is both good and not as good (note, the results are not "BAD"). A PET scan is not taking the cats for a scan to tell me how I'm doing thank you, or as one person asked me yesterday which pet was it, to which I replied a labradoodle - and seeing as we haven't had a dog in the house for 15 months, that was my attempt at some light humor. Rather, it is a positron emission tomography scan. Oh well, back to the results.

On the good news front the tumor has again gone down in size from its original "bulky" state of 4.1 x 2.5 centimeters to now being a little over 1.5 x 1.0 inches big. So I have gone from a softball or very large grapefruit to a good-sized grape (sadly not yet converted into wine for consumption - darn).

The not as good news front relates to my SUV levels (the Standardized Uptake Values, which measures activity in PET imaging and the radioactivity concentration in tumors at a point in time - no I am not a medical expert but learning the new vocabulary so Autumn and I understand what the doctor is talking about). When my first scan was taken in early September, the "score" was 18, which is very active/high and part of what led to the "aggressive" classification of my cancer. Yesterday's "score" was 4.09, well down but too active from the doctor's point of view. He is the expert so if he doesn't like it, I can't say I do.

The result of all this was an immediate walk down the hall for "Whac-A-Mole" round 6 (the doctor did not want to go any further past the end of the third week since the fifth chemo cycle). I got it done in the usual 6 hours. After getting to the Center at 7:00 for the PET scan and finishing chemo at 5:00 p.m. it was a long day.

I am now also getting two more chemo cycles, beginning January 2nd (yes three weeks between cycles) and another on January 23rd. There continues to be talk of radiation after completing the eight cycles, though the doctor has not said that is a certainty. One thing I've learned, this doctor doesn't raise things just because and so I'm mentally prepared for radiation as phase two of my treatment. The doctor also raised a possible part three yesterday which he wants to review and get a second opinion on, so I'm not going to spend too much time dwelling on that (yet). More on this option if and when it becomes a reality.

What this does mean is my hope of being cured by year's end and back to something more akin to the pre- cancer work and home life won't happen. The first travel for the year won't be the trip to Dallas for the ABI Reform Commission's Retreat or the ABI Executive Committee meeting later in February in Las Vegas; and the doctor told me not to plan on our annual March Kauai week. April and May travel are now iffy as well and it may be June before I get to resume my "flapping happy" exercises for work and for pleasure. It is what it is - my return to good health is most important.

And while I'm on the health reporting, one of the side effects from the chemo has been a case of neuropathy, primarily in my left foot. Nice to know it is chemo related, but walking on a foot that is constantly numb from the ball of the foot to the toes is a bit disconcerting. Its just part of the process and it is and will get dealt with.

Another side effect, for me at least and predictable this time around, was the lack of sleep the night after chemo (again). Yes, I was wide-awake a little after 3:00 this morning and out of bed at 4:00. The girls had to wait for their breakfast until 5:00 (poor deprived things).

81

So, the long and the short of things is my fight continues - the tumor is fighting back and my journey will now be much longer than I had hoped. The optimist is now learning to also be a realist. It may take upwards of a year to get completely healthy and if that is the case, so be it. There is only one acceptable result and that is being cancer free. There remains light at the end of the tunnel - the tunnel is just longer. There will be plenty of time for golf and other things that have been put on hold for now.

Now with the Holidays in full swing and the twelve days of Christmas upon us, I thought it appropriate to share a reminder of the Holiday spirit. No, not some charity in need as we know there are thousands of good causes. Rather a thought as we get ready to share good times with friends, family and co-workers.

Angels are everywhere; we just have to know where to look.

I've learned to look "outside the box" and see more angels than I thought existed; and I've been touched by many. I've tried to learn from my fight to be more receptive to others needs and maybe that has made me an angel for them. No doubt I will find more angels and my Christmas wish to all is that you too are touched by angels, whether you know them today or find them tomorrow and that the spirit of the Holidays lives throughout the year for you.

Thanks for your continued reading of my musings and your support. The sun will come up shortly and I'm vertical. It will be a good day.

December 15th A.M.

December 15, 2013

A pretty good day yesterday all things considered. Got the Neulasta shot late morning and being so close to the Palm Springs Street Fair, we stopped by for a couple of tamales to take to my mom for Christmas (by special request) and some Parmesan crisps for some friends for tasting before a baby shower that's coming up (no not Arielle's). Then a few errands to find a cleaners, a car wash and the usual type of things. A bite to eat and a good nap ensued.

Last night we saw "Dave Koz and Friends" in concert - a wonderful show filled with Christmas music and some of his more popular tunes. The best part was enjoying it with friends Paul and Lisa and making it through the entire show without crashing. I did that as soon as we got home.

Today will be anybody's guess as it is the second day post chemo and the first post the Neulasta shot. This typically is the hang on day so I don't expect to press my luck too much. Experience tells me "not a great idea".

I'm also getting more comfortable, if that is the right description, with the fact that my cure is a much longer-term process than I had hoped. But the cure is the goal and embracing that is more important than being upset over how long it takes. Patience has to be re-embraced, so it is. Sure, I'd like to be in full control of things but I realize beating cancer is mine to do, but the doctors to control. So today is another day towards that end result, one day closer and another day behind me.

The sun is coming up and I'm vertical. It will be a good day.

December 16th A.M.

December 16, 2013

Yesterday was about as expected post Neulasta shot - a day to feel pretty crappy and hang on. This is one of the few "predictable" parts of chemo cycles and it lived up to prior expectations. I've described this day as a hang on day and that really is how it feels. My energy level is lower than low and even taking a shower leaves me ready for a snooze.

That however did not stop Autumn from getting me out of the house for a few hours, just so I wasn't house/couch bound all day. Getting out of the house does make a difference. It was an early evening (ah dah!) but still, a good day all in all.

The longer-term course of treatment to get cured is still taking a bit of time to get my arms around. It is disappointing in that I had hoped that I'd be so much closer to being cured by the end of the year, but that was certainly now an overly optimistic view from my back porch. Reality is what it is and this too, once fully processed, will be just part of the fight and the return to good health. There is only one answer and that is to fight with everything I have to be cancer free, whatever it takes and however long it takes. Period. Any other result is just plain unacceptable.

Least anyone taking the time to read these musings thinks every day is 1000% upbeat, I wish it were so. But I fight to make every day as positive as I can, so my immune system can work in conjunction with the chemo drugs and everyone's prayers, thoughts, good wishes and HUGS, to help me get cured. The fact that my cancer chooses not to go quietly in the night is just part of my personal battle. Many others fight these fights every day too.

And as if I needed a reminder of that last fact, I looked at the Turning Heads Project website this morning and saw stories of more people dealing with their personal battles and how the ladies at the Turning Heads Project touched them like they did me. How about being 25 years old and finding out you have cancer, or a second time breast cancer patient at 40. I am one of way too many people fighting cancer, but we all take our battles to heart and know that anything less than giving ourselves every chance to beat this disease is denying ourselves a chance to live. So there really is no other acceptable choice.

Today is a new day. The sun is up and I'm vertical. It will be a good day. I hope yours is too.

December 19ᵗʰ A.m. 206.6

December 19, 2013

Well, I had the best of intentions of sitting down to write this morning and the morning has gotten away from me and it is now nearly noon. Could be a lot worse. For certain, the sun is out and I am most definitely vertical. A little work, some address catching up and a shower and where did the time go?

The effects of cycle 6 are slowly retreating into (not so) distant memories, though I am having to watch the cumulative effects of the chemo, the drugs and for me, the usual side effects. Such is the life of cancer patients and being one, I too live with these fun and games. I can report that the mustache continues to survive, though yet a bit thinner than in the past. How and why I have no idea.

Tuesday became a bit problematic when I thought I was feeling fairly decent only to leave the house to find zero, nada, none, no strength in my legs. Talk about scaring Autumn. We had errands to run and getting from the car to any of our stops was "charming" (her new favorite word). Wow, was that a shock. The good news is that seems to have now passed, though I stayed close to home yesterday except for our weekly bocce ball game last night, and even that I was very careful.

The better part of Tuesday was the chance to catch up with friends (by phone but still) that I hadn't talked to since I was diagnosed, as well as others who I've had better contact with. Those conversations mean a lot and add a spark to what can be tougher days (like Tuesday was trying to be). I am still amazed the number of people whom I have touched throughout my life, who have reached out in support. As I have said before, it is very humbling and rewarding all at the same time.

I have also found people who have gone through the possible third procedure my doctors are talking about and while I will still defer more on that procedure here and for now, knowing there are people I know who have dealt with this and come out the other side more than in one piece is very comforting.

I'm still dealing with the fact that my tunnel of cure can be another five months long, but the light shines at its end and as I have said from the beginning, there is no acceptable alternative except being cancer free when this is over. I'm not sure where the last five months have gone, or how fast the next five months may go, but I will come out the other side - count on it!

Looking forward, Michelle flies out tomorrow night so our family will be together shortly for the first time in a year, something I think we all are looking forward to. We will catch up with her on Tuesday, but being in Southern California will work too. Arielle and Ryan will head to Cincinnati on Christmas morning and Michelle will come out to the Desert for a few days and that will be good. Each little bit makes the day brighter and while to live, we need to laugh, smile and even cry, it will be a good time.

So please know that I won't give in, the delay in being where I wanted to be (cured) or anything else will beat this (bald still) guy. Thanks for continuing to care and follow my musings and progress. The sun is shining, I'm vertical and it is a good day.

December 21st A.M.

December 21, 2013

Tis the weekend before Christmas and all through the house, not even a mouse is stirring (no, its not *that early* just me). The shopping is done and wrapping too, so the rush of the Holidays will not be felt by us, just the stockings hung by the chimney with care.

The quiet of early morning remains one of the best times for me to reflect on where I am and where I need to get. Yes, I would truly have hoped to be cancer free by now, but reality worked out differently. So I deal with my daily needs to get rid of the alien life form trying its best to make my body its home. Whatever the path before me, with its highs and lows, will be dealt with head on.

I'm now into the second week post chemo cycle 6th's beginnings and at least this morning, I awoke feeling a bit more like my post chemo self than the first week has been. Simply put, the past week has been cruddy - little energy, less appetite and a general malaise. Maybe the start of this second week is better because the family is now all in the same general vicinity for the first time in a year. Whatever the reason, I will take the better feeling and soon I hope better appetite and look forward to Christmas Eve when we are all together.

So onto the day, the sun rising with whatever the day may bring, all to be dealt with as best I can, being vertical and trying to enjoy each and every moment (okay, almost every moment as there are a few times when "shit happens").

May the Holiday Weekend be filled with sunshine, being vertical (like me) and be a good day for all.

December 23rd A.m.

December 23, 2013

Expectations - to look forward to; regard as likely to happen; anticipate the occurrence or the coming of. Darn if expectations don't get in the way of reality.

Mine was thinking that the six rounds of chemotherapy would be my ultimate cure and that I could *look forward to* resuming a somewhat more "normal" work life. Obviously I was very mistaken in that expectation.

I've spent the better part of the last week dealing with the need, not only to revise my expectations, but to reduce if not eliminate them altogether and just let the healing process take place. That is not an easy thing for those of us used to being much more in control of things than we are in health related things. Oh how frustrating is that!

I certainly don't like being dependent on others and feel very much at a loss. Not that I can't and don't trust my doctors, because I do.

Nor does the need to lean on friends mean I am less of a person; I'm not. Its not being the rock for my family and friends, needing their almost continuous and daily support and knowing that there was nothing I did or could do to prevent being in this position. Talk about the ultimate in not being in control.

But this is life and we take what comes as best we can. I'd love to be more in control of my daily affairs rather than trying to survive to see tomorrow (maybe not THAT bad but you get the point), but that is not what was dealt me. When this is over and done, I will regain more control.

What is also readily apparent is that the lines of communication between Autumn and me remain as strong as ever. We both need that reassurance that we are not dealing with the stress of illness just because. Sure it would be easy to say the right thing throughout, but we know each other too well to accept platitudes without suspicion and therefore we don't go there.

She will get her time to unwind - a time I try to make come sooner versus later; but then reality strikes and I'm reminded I don't control this process so I revert back to trying to manage my expectations and accept my need to rely on others. Seems almost to be a circular argument back at me doesn't it.

We got out to see American Hustle yesterday afternoon. Interesting movie to say the least. A light dinner afterwards that had been preceded by a morning and early afternoon of cleaning the house so it was a good day. I'm still not feeling anywhere near where I have been physically (cycle 6 has been hard to get through - no surprise, just frustrating) and the neuropathy in my feet makes balance "interesting" - I've never been accused of being that light on my feet to begin with. The peanut gallery need not comment.

89

And so I am another day farther through the black hole of cancer; one day further along; one day closer to being cancer free. I don't know all that today brings, just that - the sun is (now) up and I'm vertical. It will be a good day.

Christmas Eve A.M. 206.4

December 24, 2013

T'was the day before Christmas and all through our homes, everyone was racing to finish with care the Holiday spirit. We too will join in that fun as the family comes together for the first time in a long time without the use of Face Time or some other electronic means.

To everyone who has taken the time to read these musings as I go through this journey, thank you and may all your Holidays and Christmas be filled with the joy and spirit of the Holidays.

To the Tan Man, fill the room with your smile on your first Christmas and may everyone revel in the miracle of your life and strength of being. To those who lost loved ones this year, may the loss be tempered with the joy of memories past. To everyone, remember that life brings us much to embrace and those are what keep us looking to tomorrow.

As for me, I have much to embrace, much to love and much to look forward to. With thanks for the continued support, prayers, HUGS, and however people take a moment to remember me and my fight with cancer, know that the sun is up, I'm vertical and the next couple of days will be good for me, the family and all of you.

Have a Merry Christmas or however you take stock of life today and tomorrow. Geoff

December 28th P.M.

December 28, 2013

Finishing up a whirlwind few days and I will be calling it an earlier evening than the past few days. We went into Buena Park on Christmas Eve to spend the afternoon and evening as a big family - Michelle, Arielle, Ryan, Autumn, me and my mom. Dinner with Kim and Chuck and their family capped the full family time, brief as it was.

Christmas morning broke very sunny and Autumn, Michelle and I took my mom back home, while Arielle and Ryan flew to be with his family for a few days. A drive back to Palm Desert and Christmas day was almost behind us.

We have enjoyed having Michelle with us since then, learning about Crossfit, Paleo and all that has been filling her life. She still moves at a pace that I for one, even when healthy, let alone now, have a hard time keeping up with. But we manage (somehow).

Today after taking Michelle to and picking her up from Crossfit was spent walking the College of the Desert Street Fair. Think more like a swap meet than a street fair, but the Italian sausage with sauerkraut and grilled onions was darn good.

I'm now two weeks plus since chemo cycle 6 and next Thursday I get to start the New Year with cycle 7. While I'm feeling better generally, the neuropathy in my feet hasn't improved despite the reduced dosage of <u>Vincristine Sulfate</u> (Oncovin - the "O" in R-CHOP) so that has made things interesting, or in Autumn's words, "Charming". I have to be very careful as I walk, as I am never quite sure whether my feet are truly beneath me and ready to support my still 200 plus pounds. I'm still down about 10-15 pounds from my starting weight, but because I refuse not to eat, my weight loss has probably been less than it might be otherwise. At least I'll assume that is the reason.

We go back to a bit less hectic schedule Monday after taking Michelle back to LAX for her flight to Detroit tomorrow night. Some catch up Monday morning and a hopefully quiet and uneventful drive back before getting ready for a reasonably quiet New Year's Eve "celebration" with friends down the street.

As I look back on 2013, I had so many positives that the onset of my cancer is not the most telling thing. The outreach from friends from so many walks of my life, their support and kindness, far outweigh the cancer itself. Don't get me wrong, the cure for my cancer is no fun and more often than not has left me physically drained.

Emotions have run the gamut from the deepest valley to the top of the world as I make progress. Yes, I wish I were cancer free right now but I'm not and so I go into 2014 again with the goal to be cancer free - whatever it takes and however long it takes.

May 2014 bring much good to us all. Happiness, friendship, love, laughter and just enough melancholy to enrich our lives from the good we enjoy.

For now, the sun was up today and will be tomorrow; I was and will be vertical tomorrow and these have been good days.

New Year's Eve A.M.

December 31, 2013

The year will finish off with one more test - a heart echo exam later this morning. Dropped in yesterday afternoon so as to be completed before my next doctor's appointment, which of course is on Thursday, so little time to do anything but say "no problem". While I don't think there is an issue with my "heart", the doctor of course wants to make sure my heart is withstanding the rigors of the chemo cycles and that that may lie in store for me in 2014. So off I go in an hour or so.

Yesterday I was reminded just how lucky I am compared to many others, having heard from friends whose families have their own fights before them. It is especially hard to be a parent, watching your child suffer through illness and wanting so desperately to take their place, though that would cause the child a different type of pain, watching their parent suffer. In one instance, having a child who continues their fight with CF and now facing a second lung transplant brings much angst to their parents; but their parents are by their side as they have been throughout. Others face multiple cancer tumors and less optimist outcomes than mine but they fight on with the support of their families. So I have much to be thankful for in comparison and feel badly that there is so much left to be discovered to prevent this type of disease and the accompanying anguish on friends and family.

Beyond that, I look forward to the New Year and the end of the cancer that has called my body home. It is with this as my goal and caring for my friends who face these same or very similar battles, that I wish you all a very HAPPY NEW YEAR.

Yes, the sun is up, I'm vertical and it will be a good day that ends this year and rings in 2014.

January 2, 2014 A.M.

January 2, 2014

Yes, the New Year is now into its second day and the football games will slowly wind down (not counting the NFL games this weekend of course). I hope your Year starts out slowly, without too much commotion.

Belated birthday wishes to Lisa (a New Year's Eve "kid") and to Terese, (a January 2nd birthday) who has had enough to deal with over the last few months with the sudden loss of her husband. Her's is another reminder of my fortunes - certainly not what I might want but better than many others.

For me, this January 2nd is simple – "Whac-A-Mole" cycle 7.

So with that, I begin this year's continuation of the process of extracting the unwanted alien form trying to make my body home. We've been through this a few times already so no surprises here. I will also get the results of the heart echocardiogram and what is next in the doctor's bag of treatment tricks that he does or likely has in store for me. Reports on that will follow.

But for now, the sun is coming up, I'm vertical (at least until I lie down for the chemo treatment) and it will be a good day.

January 3rd A.M. 217.0

January 3, 2014

The early morning, pre-sunrise, morning after chemo remains in effect and I sit at my desk at this early (just after 3:00 a.m.) hour as

I have for now each of the seven chemo treatments. This predictable side-effect is just another part of the getting well process and with the New Year now upon us, I have things to catch up on and the early hour isn't that offensive.

The chemo treatment itself yesterday went as the others have, without much in the way of issues during the treatment. No, I did not eat a *Turkey Sandwich* as remains on the not allowed in my treatment room list, or the house for that matter. Please don't fear that I am wasting away for that is anything but the case.

I managed to GAIN 10 pounds since my last treatment on December 16th, a feat I attribute to a) continuing to eat at least three times a day whether I am hungry or not, b) not really caring what it is I am eating, so "balanced" meals are not always the rule of thumb (yeah to ice cream, smoothies, chocolate etc.) and c) the supplies of chocolate, ham, turkey, cheese and the "fixings" that arrived on our doorstep over the Holidays (with thanks to the Ohio clan, Bob, Allan and others for those "goodies"). For those of you concerned that I might waste away, fear not. I will lose five to ten pounds after this cycle runs its course and I will begin to be a bit more careful in balancing what I eat, but I will continue to eat as best I can three meals a day, I promise. I believe this has been a factor in how I have managed this fight so far.

Another issue no doubt has been my inability to walk as much or as well as I would like care of the neuropathy (now) in both feet. My balance has been affected to some degree and my pace has been slowed both by the neuropathy and the time it has taken to recover from each successive cycle. All reasonably predictable, but it means I need to keep up the fight to feel stronger each day and take advantage of those bits of regained energy/strength and push myself just a bit further. Again, I promise nothing over-the-top or stupid, plus I have Autumn to make sure I don't do that! I did get out on a beautiful Sunday (sorry those of you suffering throughout the snow and freezing temperatures) and took a mile plus walk in the morning and a round on the 18 hole putting course here in the community with a friend - thanks Bob. A great time and it was good to get out and enjoy the fresh air before chemo cycle 7.

The results of the heart echocardiogram were very encouraging to the doctor - my heart remains strong and is handling the chemo cycles well. It seems that my body has adapted well to handling the treatments and the lack of significant side effects (if we ignore the earlier constipation and resulting fainting episode) is a good thing.

Next up is a second opinion/consultation with the doctors at the City of Hope (www.cityofhope.org) to discuss a treatment protocol that my doctor in Palm Springs believes is an important step in beating my cancer. As with his previous talking about treatments, he has now talked about the possibility of this protocol twice so I take it to have gone from a maybe to an almost certainly. Once I drive out to Duarte, CA where the main City of Hope campus is located and have the consultation, we will know better the likelihood of going ahead with this protocol. Simply put, the process harvests one's own stem cells, then you get a mega dose of chemo, after which you have your previously harvested stem cells transplanted back into your body to rebuild your immune system. Not quite as frightening as I first imagined after doing a little reading and talking with a couple of folks, one of whose wife's went through this procedure years ago for her cancer and five years later remains in remission and cancer free (thanks again Rob). The procedure is a hospital stay throughout. As I said, more on this after the second opinion-consult with the doctors at the City of Hope, which should happen between next week and the 22nd, when chemo cycle eight is tentatively scheduled. After that I'm told radiation follows.

More on that I'm sure later.

So the New Year and my road to recovery is again front and center in my/our life. As this road continues, I continue to come to grips with the need to put my health first and as hard as that has been there are no questions that it has to be. I will not give into to this cancer and it will be unceremoniously escorted out of its unwilling host (me). It just is taking more time and more treatments than I thought / wanted / hoped / expected / whatever. So be it.

Later this morning is the follow up Neulasta shot and then hunkering down to get through the tougher days post chemo. I'm now a reasonably old hand at this process so I'm ready for what comes. Plenty of (hopefully good) football to watch at an opportune time.

Thanks for continuing to follow my and my travails. That said, the sun will come up later this morning, I'm already vertical and it will be a good day. I hope yours is as well.

January 5ᵗʰ A.M.

January 5, 2014

As with prior cycles, the day after the Neulasta shot is not one of my favorites. I managed to get out of the house for the better part of the day but not without paying a price. Autumn and I played Couples Golf in the morning (a very large turnout and a slow round), and were paired with friends from Autumn's bowling and the Wednesday night bocce ball game - that was fun. Plus, Autumn had her first hole-in-one on our last hole. A hole-in-one pays $5, which meant our round was net "free".

We went out in the afternoon and picked up our bread makers from one of the local casinos and stayed out for a while. Unfortunately my energy level, coupled with a very grumpy stomach (not something I have had to deal with often thankfully) left me less than hungry and for once really not only not hungry but really not able to get anything but pills in me for dinner.

This is usually the toughest post chemo day so I'm looking forward to today, being one day removed from yesterday, to be significantly better (even if that is in degrees as no, I don't want to do a 5K today). The sun will be up shortly, I'm vertical and it will be a good day.

For those of you in the Midwest and East, stay warm and safe.

January 7th A.M. 213.0

January 7, 2014

Yes, it's another early morning. Seems this last chemo cycle has been a bit of a "dusy" and I'm a bit the worse for wear as a result. My appetite has taken a relative leave of absence, as has any reasonable semblance of sleep. For anyone who thinks any of this is fun, let me suggest otherwise.

The good news is there is plenty of life left in me and while waking up at a very unreasonable hour and having the brain kick in is not high on my daily to do list, I have taken advantage of the "extra" hours in the day and gotten through my morning routine a bit earlier than usual, so more time to read a book, currently "Wheelmen", the story behind the demise of Lance Armstrong.

It is interesting in reading this story how we so often find ways to idolize those about whom we think we know more than a bit about. Lance's story is epic, a testicular cancer survivor etc. His treatment, while not exactly similar to mine, was four cycles long and per the book, approximately four hours each. Lance of course survived his cancer and went on to accomplish what we thought were great "achievements". His though were tainted by deception, ego and some could say sheer avarice.

I have now gone through seven chemo cycles, each lasting between five and a half to six hours. Again, no comparison, but my total time getting my treatments is now almost double Lance's. Again, different cancer, different treatment. But what we thought made Lance so special is really more a reality of the world of cancer.

We each suffer through the rigors of treatment, in our own distinct ways. We can be made to be a hero for undergoing treatment or we can face our realities head on and accept that which lies before us, a long road of treatment and recovery.

I prefer to look at Jim Valvano's philosophy at dealing with his ultimately unsuccessful battle with cancer - "don't give up, don't ever give up". I'll take that with me each day, along with my definition of success, based on Coach John Wooden, that if I have given each day my very best, then I have been successful. And no one can take that away from me.

No, I'm not perfect nor is my battle extraordinary. I am one of thousands dealing with life's infirmities (I heard from a business acquaintance just yesterday that his brother had been found with bladder cancer that had spread to his spine, just another example of how much there is still to learn about cancer so as to prevent it from finding more victims). But I strive to keep my head high, my morals in tact and remember that I am but one of too too many people dealing with cancer daily. I will let that speak for me as it is much more in tune with my life, and me than the need for self-aggrandizement in the public's eye.

The sun will be up shortly and I am vertical (and probably a bit warmer than may across the country too); it will be a good day.

January 9th A.M.

January 9, 2014

Another day, another round of waiting for the multiple doctor groups to coordinate their schedules (mine obviously is less important because I'm the patient). I could yell and scream, but I doubt that will change much. So I will call Dr. Camacho's office again this morning to have them talk to the City of Hope. Grumble.

Yesterday Autumn got to take off to enjoy a night of Bunco with the La Mirada ladies. A good chance for her to take a bit of a break from the daily rigors of dealing with fighting my cancer. I of course really don't get that chance to any degree because the cancer, the chemo and everything that I deal with follow me everywhere I go. Sure, it would be great to leave everything behind even for an hour or two, but the best I can do is deal as best I can with the mental aspects of this fight and know that until I am cancer free, this is my reality.

I had a wonderful afternoon taking an hour-long walk with our friend Lisa at the indoor track at the clubhouse near the house. Great conversation, friendship and exercise. Of course post walk was a 45-minute NAP. And that is a surprise - probably not. Bocce last night and then back to the house to try to eat a little bit and then get a good night's sleep.

So another day is upon me, working my way one day closer to beating this alien and unwanted visitor. The sun is up, I'm vertical and it will be a good day. May yours be too.

January 11th A.M.

January 11, 2014

First, to start the morning a Happy 90th Birthday to my mother. Her parents lived into their nineties so her making it to this milestone should be no surprise. Her party is later today with many of her friends and some family coming to share in this day with her.

Sadly, as fate would reign on me, my body decided yesterday to throw a fever at me for the first time since starting chemo in mid-September. 102 is no fun and even less when your immune system has been thumped by now seven chemo cycles. I was able to get the fever down back under 99, only to spike up to 101, back down, back up. You get the picture. A call to the doctor and a new round of antibiotics was ordered late in the afternoon. This morning broke with me at 101.2 at 5:00 and after some liquids, Tylenol and a robe while in bed, its back down a bit.

What it means for me is not making Mom's birthday party as I can't risk the two plus hour ride/drive each way while running a fever (even I am not *that* stupid - hard headed maybe, but not that stupid). Plus Autumn would never let me consider doing more than being close to the bed - period, as was my lot yesterday, likely most of the day today and probably tomorrow too.

This is just another reminder that I am not in control of things and must listen to the doctors, Autumn and my body. I'd tell you its frustrating, but in reality its just part of dealing with cancer and treatments to be cured. Frustration comes too close to negativism, which as those who have read this throughout know is counter-productive and an inhibitor to the immune system trying to work to cure us. So frustration, like negative thoughts, can stay outside the front gate of the house - period.

So today I will spend my time helping my body fight whatever is causing the fever, watch some football and think of my Mom's celebration. With the sun being up and my being vertical, it is still a good day. Hope yours is too.

January 13th A.M.

January 13, 2014

A new week and a new round of things as this journey continues. While I missed my mother's party, all reports are that she had a truly wonderful time enjoying her friends and family. I couldn't have wanted more for her and my disappointment in not physically making the event was small versus taking care of my (now obviously a bit more) fragile health.

I seemed to turn a corner yesterday, with a full day of not having a temperature in triple digits. Yippee! Of course the thrashing of the last couple of days leaves me feeling like I'm back at the early stages of the chemo cycles and the days of Wylie E. Coyote versus Acme Manufacturing. We all know who won those battles.

I'm now waiting for the City of Hope to follow up last week's patient information call to schedule my appointment for the second opinion/consult. I've been promised that appointment will take place before January 22nd when chemo cycle ("Whac-A-Mole") session 8 is scheduled. We'll see but knowing how my doctor out here feels, if it doesn't happen, someone other than me will hear about it - loudly. So I expect it will happen. Once it does, I'll be able to talk about what may be in store with a bit more than speculation.

Today will be more rest and recovery (sorry not rest and relaxation) so as to get ready for what is next in store, whatever that may be. Some quiet time for reading, a bit of home and office work and whatever the day holds in store.

The sun is up, I'm vertical and it will be a good day.

January 15th A.M. 210.3

January 15, 2014

Finally felt well enough from last weekend's viral (I don't know what else to call it) attack to get out of the house yesterday. Took a walk in the morning and with the Santa Ana winds blowing we had spring like conditions here. Sorry all you Midwest, Ohio Valley and East Coast folks still dealing with snow and cold.

Then we got the chance to have a really fun dinner with Craig and Sarah Stuppi before they return to the Bay Area this morning. As they have a home about 3 miles from us, those dinners will be a bit more often than once every 10-15 years.

Autumn returned from her travel to Las Vegas and the internment of her mother's ashes so that particular chapter is now behind her. As has been chronicled a bit previously, the second half of the Berman's year was a bit stressful between my being diagnosed with cancer, my mom falling and breaking an arm and Autumn's mom succumbing to her third bout with cancer (two breast and the final one lung). Needless to say, we take things pretty much one-day at a time.

Today is the second opinion/consult at the City of Hope (www. cityofhope.org). Really not much more to say about that until the blood draw and doctor visit is done so my next post should hopefully be a bit more "revealing". No, there will not be film at 11!

Until then, the sun is up, I'm vertical and it will be a good day. May it be for you as well.

January 16th P.M. ▓▓▓▓▓▓▓▓▓▓▓▓▓▓▓▓

January 16, 2014

The City of Hope consult/visit/second opinion was done yesterday and while I would love to be flip, I'm not in that place at the moment. So here are the facts as best I know them (as things seem to be changing on me with a moment's notice).

The R-CHOP protocol that I've been undergoing is supposed to kill its targeted cancer within six cycles. My cancer as you know has chosen not to be so accommodating as to go away within the normal protocol. This means that I have obtained a partial remission but not full and complete remission. So an autologous stem cell transplant is now the next step in my treatment and hopefully cure.

This stem cell transplant has been done over 10,000 times by the City of Hope and therefore is not an unknown or untested procedure. I keep learning of people who have undergone this treatment and come out the other side just fine and I've been told I will as well. The process however will not be easy or in any way fun.

Next up and the beginning of the preparations for the transplant itself will be chemo cycle 8. This time instead of the R-CHOP I will be getting R-ICE, a different combination of drugs. This is done over four days (all hospitalized here in the Desert) followed by the regular Neulasta shot.

After that, and again timing is very much unknown, will be four days of shots to build up the white blood cell count, then harvesting the stem cells, then the mega dose of chemo and finally the reintroduction of the harvested stem cells. The chemo and reintroduction will be done at the City of Hope (private room but not the boy in the bubble concept). Once everything is back to the doctor's definition of normal, I will get to go home. And then there will likely be radiation for a number of weeks. When that is all done, then I hope I get a clean bill of health.

So that's what we know - much ahead of me. Much grappling with emotions, treatments, cures and knowing that there are thousands of pioneers before me and undoubtedly many more behind me.

I will post more as I learn it but know that while I have the option of saying no to this, that really isn't an option. It has been rejected. I will put my head down, face each day as it comes and deal with its consequences.

The sun is out (and a pleasant 83 degrees), I'm vertical and it is a good day.

January 20th A.M.

January 20, 2014

A new week and new challenges. This morning will be filled with the ever-changing schedule as there is much to do in advance of the stem cell transplant and as of last Friday night, the schedule was very much in flux. I am waiting for more detail from the folks at the City of Hope this morning but it sounds like tomorrow I'll be admitted to the City of Hope (versus in the Desert as I had originally been told) for the eighth round of chemo (R-ICE versus R-CHOP) which is a multi-day treatment, plus a series of tests required before the transplant process can begin in earnest. At this point, it is what it is and I will deal with things as they sort out.

After this week's treatment/tests, I'll have the usual Neulasta shot, a "class" back at the City of Hope for dealing with a Hickman catheter (used for the harvesting of the stem cells, any necessary blood transfusions and then the re-introduction of the harvested stem cells), a series of Neupogen shots to stimulate the growth of white blood cells, followed by the actual transplant process (hospitalization - chemo and reintroduction off the harvested stem cells). The entirety of the process is likely to run into early - to - mid-March. So there is much ahead of me.

I wish I could tell everyone that I'm super excited - but that just isn't the case. I've gotten more comfortable with what lies ahead of me especially considering the City of Hope has performed over 10,000 of these transplants since 1976. That by itself is very comforting. From there I will just take things as they come.

I continue to take my strength from the knowledge I will survive this and come out healthy on the other side, that friends remain concerned and care as to how I'm doing throughout this and of course, family, all of whom are there for me as I for them.

The sun is up and I'm vertical, so today will be a good day. Maybe a bit trying of a day, but a good day none the less.

January 21st A.M.

January 21, 2014

Today begins the preparation for the transplant and it's off to the City of Hope for yet another round of chemo and a series of tests. A different form of fun.

The sun is up, I'm vertical and it will be a good day.

January 23rd P.M.

January 23, 2014

Welcome to the City of Hope. I was admitted Tuesday evening after an out patient visit with my doctor and a bone marrow aspiration. This one was done under a local (think root canal as it's about the same). Then after waiting a while for a room to open up, I was sent up to my room and got as comfortable as one can. Considering that I had never spent a night in a hospital, it was a very different feeling. My first batch of chemo (more Rituxan) was initiated just before midnight. Made for a tough night of sleep. Can't say Autumn slept much better on the chair/bed but it was good to have her with me.

Yesterday was more chemo drugs and another first, a blood transfusion, as my counts were apparently below where the doctor wanted them. The incoming blood was colder than I imagined so a couple of blankets got added to the bed to keep me warm. A few more tests were done just for good measure too. Arielle came by and spent some time with me during the late afternoon/early evening. We had a good time and laughed a lot. We even walked the halls a bit for some "exercise".

Today has been more of the same, with a CT scan thrown in for good measure as the doctor is watching something in one of my lungs. Nothing to worry about so I'm told. Okay so I won't worry. I've been visited by a clinical psychologist, a social worker, a physical therapist and a host of folks all of who are part of the "team" for transplant patients. They try to cover everything believe me.

Otherwise, it's rest, read, watch a little golf, answer e-mails as they come through (the wireless here needs a major upgrade) and sleep. So for those of you worried that I'm not putting my health first, have no fear, that is almost all I'm doing. The sun was up and I'm still vertical (well sort of at the moment) and it's a good day. May yours be good as well.

January 25th lunchtime

January 25, 2014

My stay at the City of Hope got extended through the weekend when the CT scan revealed a spot on my right lung. So in the middle of the four days of chemo and the 24-hour ifosphomide drip, I had a bronchoscopy. The results so far are good; the spot is not cancer; the spot is likely bacterial or fungal in nature and I've been getting meds to address this on top of the chemo. That (The Chemo) is now behind me. The shots follow and hopefully I will get to go home Monday. I know however I will be back when the transplant takes place.

The sun is out and I get vertical during the day, so it's a good day. Photos will be added at some point.

January 26th P.M Late evening

January 26, 2014

A day full of ups and downs.

Last night I thought I had had a cup of decaffeinated (Orange Spice) tea. Quite good, but sadly NOT decaffeinated. So you can image just how well I slept, especially when added to my Lasik pill and all the fluids I get intravenously. My I.V. From Tuesday night, which was hard enough to get in, gave up the ghost this morning and after a blood draw and two tries, another nurse had to come to place a new I.V. in the vein in the top of my right hand. Can you say ouch?

The weekend doctor came by and there was no news re the spot on my lung; Petrie dishes are being cultured and tests run but no news other than they don't think the lesion is cancer. I'll take that's good news. Autumn wasn't feeling great and as she was dealing with sinus issues, it was better for her to stay home today, which of course was a disappointment. I had a good visit with our friend Kim, who came with Arielle. Arielle was here most of the day and had a good run at gin rummy, which she is starting to understand.

The breaking point was when I ordered a grilled cheese sandwich for lunch, only to have food service call me back saying they were out of white bread. Murphy was an optimist rules yet again. It was so ridiculous it was funny and my mood lightened for sure. I also had a really wonderful nurse today (thank you Sherry) not that they all aren't good, but today was extra special. She really helped me through the day. I also met a recent transplant recipient as we both walked the halls for some exercise. It was nice to see someone on the other side, even if he is still here.

So now as evening is upon me and I head to an evening of hopefully more peaceful sleep, I know I am in great hands here; many others have gone through this and come out into their new life; I have tremendous support from family and friends and DSI (thanks Bill) and; it will get better.

The sun will come up in the morning and I will get vertical, for walks, friends and maybe, just maybe to go home. If not, okay, then we will see what Tuesday brings. May tomorrow be filled with good things for each of you and thanks again for staying up with my journey.

January 27th evening (really this time)

January 27, 2014

Good news, my lung issues were determined to be such that I was released from the hospital tonight. Yippee and yeah. I got the news around 12:30 this afternoon and while it took a while, once Autumn got there and dealt with the pharmacy for the latest additions to my pharmacopeia, a few instructions for my upcoming shots, and off we went.

I don't have much in the way of restrictions before Sunday, when I return for the harvesting of my stem cells. That is out-patient and

I will get to return home before the mega chemo and transplant. So yes, it's been a very good day. We're enjoying Arielle and Ryan's company tonight before heading home.

The sun was up today and will be tomorrow (sorry Chicago and east as you freeze again), I was and will be vertical and it will be a good day.

January 30th A.M.

January 30, 2014

It is nice to be home. After a night with Arielle and Ryan and a return to the City of Hope to pick up the remaining prescription, Autumn and I made our way back to the Desert Tuesday. All the corny sayings are true, home is where one's heart is and being able to get into our house was a huge uplift.

We also got the chance to spend a little bit of time with Adrienne Lindblad, down to help her in-laws settle into their new home in the Palm Springs area and before her flight back to Seattle. The time went all too quickly, but it was nice to catch up in person and hear how everyone in the Lindblad family is doing, and of course give her a first hand look at me and that yes, I'm still vertical and plugging along. (Apologies for the tired looking guy in this photo and the late afternoon sun. The vest is because I still can't regulate my body temperature with any regularity and I had gotten cold in the house - what do I know . . .)

Another day of catch up (both home and the office at least a little bit) yesterday followed by some fun with our friends at the District bocce ball game. As I'm getting closer to the transplant process itself, I passed on playing but enjoyed the company. More of the same today, dinner with friends and before I know it will be Sunday and back to Duarte to begin the stem cell harvesting leading up to the chemo/transplant. But again, being home is such a nice and good feeling.

For those of you who are afraid to call, please know that the chance to talk to and see friends is something both Autumn and I cherish. It helps to be able to stay in contact with friends and while I recognize, people don't want to intrude or disturb me, it's neither. Okay, I admit if I'm asleep it could be an issue, but Autumn will then usually have the phone so you'll get her, which is not a bad thing in my book; and if I've had too much that day, she will answer the phone. You win either way. Seriously, the chance to talk with friends is a big positive.

So I go into today one step closer to tomorrow, one step closer to the end of this journey, one step closer to good health. The sun is coming up and I'm vertical (thank you Shiloh for the early wake up "meow"). It will be a good day. Hope yours is too.

January 31st A.M.

January 31, 2014

A fun evening last night with Norm and Lulu at a new (for us) restaurant, Piero's Pizza Vino in Palm Desert. Good company, good food and a quiet casual way for an Italian meal.

We got caught up on a few things needing attention yesterday and are slowly gearing up for the stem cell harvesting process that begins next week back at the City of Hope. This will be the last outpatient phase before the chemo and transplant to follow. Now if the paperwork would just get in order (sorry, that is a small dig to the insurance company to *approve* this process now please). I'm still feeling a bit like a ping-pong ball bouncing between hospital, providers and the carrier. A bit of calm and coordination would be nice. I am happy to know the insurance company deems this process at the Life Support level. Gee thanks!

A bit of stress relief coming for Autumn and Arielle this weekend as well. Girls weekend away I believe is the phrase. Well deserved in my book.

Yesterday also brought a few calls from friends around the country that I haven't spoken to in a bit and as I've said before, those calls bring some uplifting to the spirits. I will get to where I say thank you in person when this is behind me.

The sun is up, though behind a cloudy start to the Desert's morning and I am vertical. It will be a good day.

February 1ˢᵗ A.M.

February 1, 2014

January went out with a few more wrinkles to the treatment plan, though for a change I really can't say its feet dragging by my insurance company. The carrier hasn't yet "approved" my stem cell transplant because they haven't gotten the results of all the tests needed for that approval and seeing as the last of the needed tests was scheduled for *next* Wednesday its hard to argue with that logic. That means everything gets shifted back at least a week (except for my getting the daily dose of Neupogen - that continues).

Along those lines, it's been a long time since I've woken up to sore knees and shins, a direct result of these shots. Takes me back to when I was 10 years old and growing like a weed. Does this mean I'll get back to 6' 6"?

Probably not and that's okay too - no wardrobe additions need be contemplated.

What the coming week holds is still therefore in flux. Thinking back to the Heinz commercial that used Carly Simon's song *"Anticipation"*, (its making me wait) is probably the best description. What I know won't happen is any stem cell collection.

For those of you hearing stories of the monster kitty, Shiloh has recently taken it upon herself to be a bit of a terror. Yesterday she started in at 3:00 A.M. with efforts to be annoying and fed. I am happy to report that she let me sleep in today to the more normal 5:15 A.M. Aren't I the lucky guy!

Spirits are rebuilding and looking forward to moving things along to clean health. The sun is out, I'm vertical and it will be a good day.

February 4ᵗʰ A.M.

February 4, 2014

The Super Bowl has come and gone and puppies, Clydesdales and eating Doritos, wins our hearts again for getting the pulse of Americana right again. Maybe some of the advertising agencies and ad buyers might take a moment to look at the message they are trying to send and re-think the edgy, not related at all to their product ads that they spend so much time and money on.

As for me, Autumn and I got to watch the game with Arielle and Ryan (thanks again Ryan for coming to get me). It may not have been real artistic, but watching a defense play to their capabilities and shut down the high octane Bronco offense was worth the full game watch.

We returned to the Desert yesterday to deal with more insurance company information requests, claims from last August that remain unresolved and other things needed to move the needle for my transplant forward.

I head back to the City of Hope tomorrow for a full day of testing and doctor visits then back home by evening's end. That is of course unless there is some change wrought upon the schedule for which I have no co control.

We will deal with that as it happens (should I say if it happens).

I want to take a moment to again take stock of my "lot" in life, at least publicly on this site. I mentioned a few weeks ago someone whose daughter had fought CF for many years. I learned yesterday that the daughter succumbed to the disease on Sunday and no doubt, while now no longer having to fight the daily fight, her parents are saddened by the loss of their daughter. I'm still very much alive and will continue my fight, as I know that I am one on so many, too many, that deal with cancers, muscular dystrophy, CF and so many other diseases. Their courage in dealing with their own pain is a reminder that giving in, for me, is not an option.

For just one example of the fight of people afflicted, see http://www. teamgleason.org, the website for former Washington State and New Orleans Saints Steve Gleason, who is fighting ALS. His motto is no white flags (no surrender) and his desire to go to Peru to the top of Machu Picchu (under the Adventures tab) was chronicled by NFL Films. It is just another reminder that our desire to live and fight each day to live it to its fullest is what matters most. It fuels our love of others, their support, their caring, sharing and joining us in how we go about living each day. Thank you to the Steve Gleason's of the world isn't enough. Living is a small way to say thanks.

So my fight continues, day by each day. The sun will be up shortly and I'm already vertical (thank you Shiloh for the attempt at a 4:30 wake up call). It will be a good day. May yours be as well.

February 5th late morning

February 5, 2014

Another day, another twist in the care and treatment protocol. I got a call late morning yesterday morning from the doctors that they had diagnosed the spot on my lung as a bacteria not all that common but for those like me, with compromised immune systems (and that's before the transplant), very risky. So with little fanfare we drove back to the City of Hope and I was admitted. Oh goody.

I got a room quite quickly but one where an extension on the bed would not work because it would hit the wall and I would not be able to get the IV pole around it. A room change followed and while about the same size, the layout is much more user (me) friendly. Then of course were the multiple tries to get IVs in (more ouches), the usual wake up for vitals, more bags of stuff and you can imagine how well I slept. Autumn was smart to go to Arielle and Ryan's so she should have gotten a decent night's sleep (comparatively speaking I would hope). I'm likely to be in the hospital through the weekend and I'll confirm, the hospital process is already wearing thin. I know, wait until the transplant. Gee thanks. :-)

Otherwise, the sun is up and after having two CT scans this morning, I'm sort of vertical. It will still be a good day.

February 7th A.M.

February 7, 2014

As I noted in my last post, the return visit was certainly not on my radar. Turns out I have pneumonia, though the bacteria in question shows up less than one percent of the time. Why should I be surprised? So it's been three days of tests, X-rays, poking, prodding, a PICC line to stop the peripheral I.V.s and today another scan. Sleep of course in a hospital is always problematic but last night the "visits" were fewer than before and I actually got some pretty decent sleep.

I'm still dealing with the concept that I haven't and still don't feel "sick" but I obviously have a lot going on in my body. There are plenty of times when doubt and fear creep in, but I try to keep those at a minimum. I walked 1.5 miles through the halls so that I can try to keep up some semblance of fitness and that too makes a big difference, as I'm not a fan of sitting in the room all day.

Today Bill and Patrice are coming by and I'm looking forward to their visit. Of course I have tests to undergo before they get here and probably a handful of doctor bedside visits. It won't be a dull day. And as I was typing, the first of the doctor visits just occurred. Unless there is a change, I'm here for a few days.

With that, I'm signing off for now. The sun is up, I've been and will be on and off through the day, vertical. It will be a good day.

February 8ᵗʰ Noon

February 8, 2014

Still enjoying the hospitality of the Helford Hospital at the City of Hope and have been told I have at least another ten days as their "guest" while I work on beating back my particular form of pneumonia. It's a good thing the nursing staff and patient care assistants are so friendly.

I walked a mile this morning with my sidekick, Mr. Pole. His sense of humor and conversation style are a bit bland and when he is upset, he "beeps". Of course he has been known to do that in the middle of the night while I'm asleep. I wish he could make up his mind.

I got some good news last night when the results of my PET scan came in. My tumor has started to give in to the eight rounds of chemo and it is almost, but not quite dead. This had the lead doctor pleased and us too. It won't alleviate the need for the transplant but I won't have the tumor to deal with too. I also had a great visit with Bill and Patrice, who also got to see Autumn and Arielle while here. They got to hear the good news as well and heard first hand that some progress has been made (yeah).

Otherwise, the routine is pretty much the same. Vitals every four hours (yes every four hours), lots of IV fluids, some company and trying to keep up with the outside world. But I can attest, the sun came up and I'm vertical, so it's a good day.

February 10th. A.M.

February 10, 2014

Happy Monday morning. Yes, I'm still sort of comfortably ensconced in the hospital as the doctors keep working on my form of pneumonia. Between the antibiotics and sugar water continuously being pumped into me, sleep is regularly interrupted by the need to empty my bladder. Add the blood draw between 3:00 - 4:00 a.m. and regular check of my vitals, sleep is very broken up. This week is more of the same, antibiotics, doctor visits and the like.

Otherwise, I'm feeling fairly decent and enjoyed the weekend visits by Arielle and Ryan and Kim and Chuck. I've been walking at least a mile every day. Mr. Pole and I make sure to have regular conversations, though he continues to only reply with "beep, beep, beep" when he chooses to reply.

I see the sun rising now and I'm vertical (at the moment sitting up so that counts), so it is a good day.

February 12th. A.M.

February 12, 2014

I've come to believe that there is some conspiracy when hospitalized that sleeping at night is to be prevented. In my case, it's either my bladder wanting attention every 90 minutes courtesy of all the fluids

I get through the multiple IVs I'm getting, or a nurse checking the IVs, a PCA wanting vital signs, or Mr. pole "beeping". Then of course you get the question in the morning "what is your fatigue level". Really? I'm great if you ignore the dark circles under my sunken eyes. On the brighter side of things, I actually am getting some sleep.

Right now I'm in a holding pattern, getting my antibiotics all throughout the day and hopefully beating back the bacteria in my lung. Progress will be determined when the next CT scan is done, though there is no date certain for that scan. So it's status quo.

The sun is up (as best I can tell out of the one window in my room) and I'm vertical, so it's a good day.

I hope each of you reading this have a good day too.

February 15th A.M.

February 15, 2014

Good morning from home. Yes, I was released from the hospital yesterday afternoon so that I can continue my recuperation from pneumonia at home. Of course, I am still on two types of antibiotics, one orally (horse pills) and one through my PICC line. I have a home health nurse coming this morning to "teach" us how to accomplish that. But it's still at home. Yeah!

The transplant process is on hold for a couple of weeks but is a necessary thing for me to get healthy, so don't think that is by the wayside. It isn't, just delayed. That is okay by me. I don't need a reoccurrence of the pneumonia or the cancer.

I've spent some time this morning catching up on things that piled up while I was in the hospital these last eleven days. Nothing too much, but its good to feel mostly caught up. So now it's on to getting some errands done, more sleep, lots of pills etc.

The sun is up, I'm vertical (and at home). It is a good day.

February 17ᵗʰ A.M.

February 17, 2014

We finally got the home health care straightened out and I am now back on track three times a day here at home. This morning's was at 4:00 a.m., which meant we both had to get up and yes, when it was done we both went back to bed. It's almost like being back in the hospital. But being home, if even for a brief couple of weeks, is an uplifting change.

The weekend brought a visit from one of my colleagues from Chicago here visiting his parents, and calls from friends. All of these bring added joy when I may be feeling a bit down (which I wasn't this past weekend). This week holds some time for rest, a visit with our friends here in Sun City and a doctor's appointment back at the City of Hope. All in all a nice, almost relaxing week.

The sun is up, I'm vertical and it is a good day. I hope it us for you as well.

Geoff Berman

February 20th A.M. ▓▓▓▓▓▓▓▓▓▓▓▓▓▓▓▓

February 21, 2014

Sorry for the recent lack of posting, but there hasn't been much to say as we muddle along with the three times a day antibiotic through the PICC line (yes, including the middle of the night/early morning one) and the oral antibiotic (also three times a day), plus a whole list of other medications. Sleep patterns are very messed up for all in the house. Only Dakota seems to be non-pulsed by the changes.

The update as far as the bacterial infection is that there is no update. Autumn and I spent a good portion of the day yesterday at the City of Hope (due in part to changes in my appointment times that I was not aware of (nor was the doctor), so we were out of the house for almost twelve hours including travel time to and from the facility. I go back next week for another CT scan of my chest to see what progress has been made in eradicating the infection. Based on that scan decisions will be made as to what to do if the infection is still there and/or timing of restarting the transplant process (one 24 hour chemo cycle, ten days of Neupogen, harvesting the stem cells and then the chemo/transplant itself).

So the news is no news until the middle of next week. Otherwise, I still feel fine, am eating as well as I can, walking as best I can courtesy of the neuropathy in my feet and focusing on getting better.

Yes, the sun is up, I'm vertical and it is a good day.

Geoff Berman

February 20th A.M. ▓▓▓▓▓▓▓▓▓▓

February 21, 2014

Sorry for the recent lack of posting, but there hasn't been much to say as we muddle along with the three times a day antibiotic through the PICC line (yes, including the middle of the night/early morning one) and the oral antibiotic (also three times a day), plus a whole list of other medications. Sleep patterns are very messed up for all in the house. Only Dakota seems to be non-pulsed by the changes.

The update as far as the bacterial infection is that there is no update. Autumn and I spent a good portion of the day yesterday at the City of Hope (due in part to changes in my appointment times that I was not aware of (nor was the doctor), so we were out of the house for almost twelve hours including travel time to and from the facility. I go back next week for another CT scan of my chest to see what progress has been made in eradicating the infection. Based on that scan decisions will be made as to what to do if the infection is still there and/or timing of restarting the transplant process (one 24 hour chemo cycle, ten days of Neupogen, harvesting the stem cells and then the chemo/transplant itself).

So the news is no news until the middle of next week. Otherwise, I still feel fine, am eating as well as I can, walking as best I can courtesy of the neuropathy in my feet and focusing on getting better.

Yes, the sun is up, I'm vertical and it is a good day.

Geoff Berman

February 20th A.M. ▓▓▓▓▓▓▓▓▓▓▓▓▓

February 21, 2014

Sorry for the recent lack of posting, but there hasn't been much to say as we muddle along with the three times a day antibiotic through the PICC line (yes, including the middle of the night/early morning one) and the oral antibiotic (also three times a day), plus a whole list of other medications. Sleep patterns are very messed up for all in the house. Only Dakota seems to be non-pulsed by the changes.

The update as far as the bacterial infection is that there is no update. Autumn and I spent a good portion of the day yesterday at the City of Hope (due in part to changes in my appointment times that I was not aware of (nor was the doctor), so we were out of the house for almost twelve hours including travel time to and from the facility. I go back next week for another CT scan of my chest to see what progress has been made in eradicating the infection. Based on that scan decisions will be made as to what to do if the infection is still there and/or timing of restarting the transplant process (one 24 hour chemo cycle, ten days of Neupogen, harvesting the stem cells and then the chemo/transplant itself).

So the news is no news until the middle of next week. Otherwise, I still feel fine, am eating as well as I can, walking as best I can courtesy of the neuropathy in my feet and focusing on getting better.

Yes, the sun is up, I'm vertical and it is a good day.

February 24th A.M. 218.7 ▇▇▇▇▇▇▇▇

February 24, 2014

We are in a holding pattern until the 26th, when I have the next CT scan, more blood work, changing the PICC line dressing and a doctor's visit for what lies in store for me next, so this post won't have anything major as to my health. As the saying goes, film at 11:00 but in this case update later in the week.

I continue with the antibiotic regimen, including the 3-4:00 a.m. dose. Fortunately, most mornings I can go back to sleep - much less of a problem for Autumn though we do have those occasional mornings when we are WIDE AWAKE. (Oh sorry.) Add the oral antibiotics, horse pills that they are, and a slew of other medications and it is a process that is for sure.

I still can't say I feel "bad". I walked 1.6 miles yesterday afternoon in 35 minutes, a bit closer to my old, pre- cancer pace, though with the still ever present neuropathy in my feet, walking is a tad tougher than it was before. It is not stopping me, just slowing me down a bit.

Had another interesting conversation with the insurance company today, who called to tell me the CT scan was approved but that there were places closer to home where I could have the scan done. Ah dah! When I asked the man on the phone why he was telling me that when the insurance company was requiring all my tests be done at the City of Hope and had he bothered to talk to the LifeSource folks, all I got was "I didn't know".

Mind boggling to say the least. Needless to say, the scan will be done at the City of Hope.

Beyond that, I was fortunate to hear from friends over the past few days, including a conversation with one of my teachers from elementary school. Our class has had reunions twice over the years and stay in touch with one another fairly well. My teacher, now in her 80's, lives outside of Pittsburgh, but remembers our class with fond and vivid memories. She adds yet another facet of my life to be concerned with my health. Wow. I'm still finding folks from my daily business world just learning of my cancer, despite my not keeping it a secret and their good wishes help every day, as does everyone who I've heard from and spoken with these past seven months.

Yes, I have more to go to be cancer free, but as I have said before, I will get to the other side and be healthy. It's just taking longer than I expected, or hoped. But the sun is out, I'm vertical and it is a good day.

Thanks for continuing to care.

P.S. Congrats to Paul and Lisa on the birth of their first grandchild, Quinn, early this morning. It's nice to have another child coming into the world to bring joy to her family. Arielle and Ryan's turn is not that far away.

March 3rd A.M.

March 3, 2014

A really nice weekend (if you ignore the ongoing 4:00 a.m. antibiotic infusion). We went to Arielle and Ryan's for a baby shower hosted by Arielle's friend Abby and her other mother Kim. A very good time and a lot of fun. Watch out for the "baby" game. We use that word in so many aspects of life besides talking about the upcoming child (such as "food baby", "baby sister" etc.) that you will lose the game in no time flat. But there were lots of laughs to accompany it.

We had to go back to the Desert right afterwards (dodging a few rain squalls) so as to be home for the 8:00 p.m. infusion, but it was good to see friends and give them a chance to see that I really am still upright and feeling good. And it was good that we got to be at the baby shower and be a part of it.

The photo is from the shower and includes Autumn's "baby" sister Terri and her husband Steve, who made the trip from the Seattle area to be a part of the festivities and my mother / Arielle's grandmother. As I said, lots of laughter and plenty of smiles too, not to mention TOO MUCH FOOD! (Yeah I know, one doesn't have to eat it just because it is there, but it was too good to pass up.)

The transplant process is now underway, with a Cytoxan session at the end of the week (11 hours worth) then restarting the Neupogen shots, leading to the harvesting process in about two weeks and the mega chemo and stem cell transplant around the end of this month. Its nice to have the process back underway and I will deal with my nerves as to parts of the process as they come up.

Otherwise, the sun is up and I'm vertical. It is a good day. I hope it is for you as well.

March 5th A.M.

March 5, 2014

One more quiet day before beginning the first phase of the transplant process. As I get reminded regularly, my health is priority number one and the quiet days are being taken advantage of as I have been sleeping later than my "norm", though that is courtesy of the 4:00 a.m. antibiotic infusion. Still, no complaints about the extra sleep.

I am able to keep my hand in work related issues, which helps me to not slip into too casual thought processes as there will be a day I get to return to my previous work world in a greater degree. I've already had a few calls this morning and it does help keep the brain stimulated for sure.

Otherwise, the sun is up and I'm vertical - it is a good day.

The picture is another from Arielle's baby shower with Arielle and her grandmother. Again, a very good time had by all.

March 8th P.M.

March 8, 2014

Back home again (no, not in Indiana) after completing the first phase of the transplant process, the one-day chemo cycle to restart the process of significant white blood and stem cell production. The eleven-hour day was without any significant issues as for whatever reason my body seems to tolerate the chemo drugs pretty well.

This was a four-hour fluid infusion, 45 minutes of pre-chemo drugs (think anti-nausea for one and Benadryl for another), two hours of Cytoxan, then another four hours of fluids. Autumn and I finished off the evening with a light Mexican meal, then back to our room on site at the City of Hope Villages for my evening anti-biotic infusion and then some sleep.

Of course, like all the other chemo cycles before it, I slept hard but woke up around 1:30 and then got up about 3:30 (quietly) until the 4:00 wake up for the next anti-biotic infusion. We got on the road back home early, with a brief stop for breakfast at one of our favorite coffee shops, Don & Sweet Sue's in Cathedral City. Catch up on some paper work, some naps (yes for both of us) and then started the Neupogen shots (those are the next phase of the pre-transplant process), all three of them I will get a day for ten days.

Next after that will be the harvesting procedure followed by the in-patient chemo, stem cell transplant and recovery. That final step will take most of April. But it will be worth it to finally be cancer free.

I hope to be sufficiently well enough by August to make our Hawaii vacation, preceded by a conference in Maui. But that is too far away to be taken as a for sure, for sure.

My spirits are good especially with the transplant process now under way. There are still some nervous / scary times ahead of me (primarily the chemo cycles and the transplant itself), but those will pass. So keeping my head up, enjoying the rest opportunities before me and the goal of finally beating this thing.

The sun has been up and its warm here in the Desert, I definitely am vertical and it is a good day. Remember to "Spring Forward" tonight but as I don't get a lot of sleep anyways, its not really an hour lost. Just sunlight gained.

For those of you who haven't been to the City of Hope and its world class facility, you can look at www.cityofhope.org to see where I am getting my care.

Thanks for continuing to be interested in my story.

March 11th A.M.

March 11, 2014

I had an interesting conversation with a friend yesterday that made me realize that my physical appearance and efforts to face my cancer head on have maybe caused me, as well as others, to minimize how "sick" I have been these past eight months or so. No, I have never assumed I wasn't "ill" or facing a foe that could kill me if ignored. But in taking the positive first, last and (almost) only approach, some facts have probably been overlooked.

According to the National Cancer Institute, the estimated number of non-Hodgkin lymphoma cases in 2013 totaled almost 70,000, with over 19,000 deaths resulting from those cases. Having been diagnosed in 2013, I'm one of the estimated new cases, but thank you, I'm definitely NOT one of the deaths.

See http://www.cancer.gov/cancertopics/types/non-hodgkin.

I've written about my upcoming stem cell transplant, but for those more interested in just what it is all about, I'd suggest if you have a few minutes to browse through the City of Hope's website on the process, at http://www.cityofhope.org/hct. There is some scary information on the recurrence of cancer in patients who go through chemotherapy only and with the expertise of the group managing my treatment and care, I expect to long outlive those who don't go through this process.

This may be an "*in your face*" way to face the reality that I have been and am still "sick", despite my not feeling bad, having nausea or many other "symptoms". But sick I have been and will be until I get through the upcoming transplant. No, I really haven't wanted to feel "sick" and am glad I haven't felt sick.

Turning to today, it's another chance to rest up for that which lies ahead of me. A few errands, a bit of "work" and of course, the three times a day antibiotic infusions to get rid of the bacterial infection that set me back a bit. Yes, I still feel good, have my head held high and am dealing with my "fears" of the unknown. Put another way, this is reality, not "reality TV" and I'm living it (as is Autumn, our family and everyone who supports me in this fight).

I can attest that yet again, the sun is out and I'm vertical. It is a good day.

March 13th A.M. ▨▨▨▨▨▨▨▨▨▨

March 13, 2014

Some good news for a change, as my doctor called yesterday to change my antibiotic. No more 4:00 a.m. infusions. Autumn was ready to jump up and celebrate but I think she was too tired. Of course one of the cats wanted to get up at 4:00 to get fed but she suffered through.

I'm still on track to get stem cells harvested beginning next Monday and then to begin the chemo/transplant process on the 31st. Every day is a day closer to getting this behind me.

I'm not always a big Dear Abby fan, but yesterday our local paper ran a column that resonated with me. The inquiry was about a column from years ago that "eloquently described the desire of the writer that his body be used to allow others to live through organ donations". The column was re-printed and can be found at http://news.yahoo.com/mans-last-wish-let-death-others-life-050011789.html and is a testament to caring for others when our time is done. "If you do all I have asked, I will live forever."

I've said many times I have much to live for and am not ready for my life to be over. But if something were to happen, I would hope that my life would be able to have meaning for others through organ donation. Call it paying it forward, but it would be a fitting way for me to move on.

The sun is up (though a bit cloudy here this morning), I'm vertical and it is a good day.

March 16th A.M.

March 16, 2014

Tomorrow begins phase two of the transplant process and Autumn and I head out this afternoon for my out- patient stay. A surgical procedure tomorrow morning to put in the Hickman catheter and take out the PICC line, followed hopefully by the first stem cell harvesting procedure. That I'm told that is a four-hour process hooked up to an apheresis machine to filter the blood for the stem cells and then return the blood back to me. Sounds funkier than it really is. Once done, I'll get to return home sometime before week's end for the last rest period before the transplant.

I have no magical words of encouragement, for me or others. This is frankly the next step in getting healthy and that is the most important thing. I still get much of my will power from friends who reach out, by e-mail, phone, a friendly meal together (thanks Norm and Lulu - hope the surprise party was fun) and those nearby who take a moment or two of their time to stop by (thanks Paul - and Lisa, feel better).

What I keep learning is that I am by no way alone in this fight. Friday night I ran into a gentleman that had recently completed his stem cell transplant at the City of Hope. Different lead doctor, but same procedure, same result - a clean bill of health. Just another reminder that way too many people are having to fight this fight and many get to the healthy side, as will I.

That said, the sun is up, I'm vertical (with some things to do around the house before heading out) and its a good day. May it be for everyone as well.

March 19th P.M.

March 19, 2014

Another phase of the pre-transplant process is now behind me, as I was able to have more than the requested / required number of stem cells harvested in just two days versus potentially much longer and therefore I was allowed to go home. There is no rhyme or reason as to why one person can have 3+ million stem cells harvested in a day and others can't get more than 500,000 in a day. I was 3.5 and 4+ million each of the last two days so I was told to go home. Now except for a treadmill stress test next Tuesday, I'm good to go on the 31st.

That schedule (an estimate only) calls for me to be admitted on the 31st, with chemo to begin on April 1st (no, its not a fool's day joke). I will be getting a round of chemo daily for seven days and on the 8th, the harvested stem cells are transplanted back into me. After that, however long it takes to get to where I can be released from the hospital so be it.

I spoke to my original oncologist this afternoon and he commented that he has never lost a patient in the City of Hope's hands. I promised not to be the first!

So knowing I am finally just around the corner from this treatment is both exhilarating and a tad scary. Either way, getting this in my rear view mirror is next on my horizon.

The sun is definitely up, I'm vertical and it is a good day.

March 20th A.M.

March 20, 2014

Many of our friends have asked throughout my battle what they can do to help and generally I have told everyone that their thoughts, prayers and good wishes are more than enough to help get me through.

As my stem cell transplant approaches, there is one thing everyone who has taken the time to follow my traverse can consider. I have been told to expect to need whole blood and platelets throughout the transplant process. Many of you are from areas outside Southern California. Directed donations for me are only possible at the City of Hope facility in Duarte, CA. However taking a moment to give blood or platelets where you work or live will give others undergoing treatment for cancer or other diseases a chance to continue in their personal battles. Call it "paying it forward", or whatever you may want, but it does make a difference.

For those of you here in the greater Southern California area that are willing to consider making a blood/platelet donation, please contact Jennifer Zuniga, Directed Donation Coordinator, Blood Donor/Apheresis Center at the City of Hope, (626 256 4673). Even if you can't or don't wish to make a donation (directed or otherwise), its okay. Your continued thoughts and prayers will be a big help to get me to the other side so this fight will be in my rear view mirror versus the front windshield.

The sun is up, its the first day of Spring (which for many means the end of a tough Winter) and yes, I'm vertical. It is a good day.

March 25ᵗʰ A.M. ▨▨▨▨▨▨▨▨▨▨▨

March 25, 2014

Headed back to the City of Hope for the next to last test before the real fun begins. Each passing day brings me one day closer to being cancer free and while there remains some trepidation as to getting through the process, I've met and spoken to enough people who have made it to the other side that I know I can and will too. Beyond that, there is little to add. My focus sharpens a bit more each day to the task ahead of me.

What doesn't change is the appreciation for family and friends, who continue to be so supportive of my fight. Being able to say thank you once cancer free, will be a wonderful thing I am looking forward to. Until then, its one day at a time, one sunrise at a time and one sunset at a time (though sadly not on Kauai this week - oh well, next year).

The sun will be up shortly, I'm already vertical and it will be a good day.

March 26ᵗʰ A.M. ▨▨▨▨▨▨▨▨▨▨▨

March 26, 2014

Last hurdle to beginning the transplant process was cleared yesterday when I "passed" the treadmill stress test. There were no grades, just pass or not, so I have no complaints about passing nor do I care what level I reached. Passing is passing, period. So now, but for the passage of a few days, it's on to the chemo and transplant.

Today would normally be spent quietly on a bluff in Princeville, Kauai with a dinner at one of our favorite restaurants on the Island.

But dealing with cancer changes things, as always, so we will stay close to home today as we celebrate our 31st Anniversary. Autumn and I have seen a lot over our years together, but the last eight months have strengthened our bond and our mutual resolve to my getting to good health. Yes, today would be spent differently if we could, but we will enjoy the day because we have the day to be together.

It's a blustery day in the Desert, but the sun will be up, I'm vertical and its a good day.

March 29th A.M.

March 29, 2014

The week is now done and I edge ever closer to beginning the transplant process and getting this behind me. As Monday comes closer, I get a bit tenser as while I generally understand what lies before me, until it is in my rear view mirror, there is some trepidation about what lies before me.

Instead of being woken up by Shiloh every morning between 3:30 and 5:00, it will be one of the nursing staff to take vitals, blood draws (and to make sure I'm breathing no doubt). Not sure which is better. The nurses however don't purr in your face or jump on the headboard so I'll let you decide.

The weekend will be for last minute things that need to be taken care of before Monday morning and the drive back to Duarte. Then a blood draw, a PET scan, a visit with Dr. Nade and wait for a bed to open up in the afternoon. Packing is easy - my electronics, a book or two, slippers, robe, and me. Clothing is not really applicable so no worries about clashing outfits, mismatched socks, etc. I'd pack a brush but then I haven't had to worry about bed hair since early October. (For those wondering about the mustache, it survived until January when I had the then 7th chemo cycle. That was its last stand. I have since brought it back to life, more salt than pepper by the way, but with seven days of chemo in a row ahead of me, it may fall back in retreat yet again. Have no fear, I will do it again when the chemo is all over.)

One of the benefits of being treated at a facility such as the City of Hope is that treatment of cancer patients is but one of its many activities. Research actually takes up a significant amount of the facility's time and resources. It also provides us with opportunities to "pay it forward" by participating in ongoing research. I will have that opportunity, as there is research into how the different types of immune cells grow and develop after a stem cell transplant. Its not hard to have an extra vial of blood drawn each time they take blood post transplant and if it helps lead to a cure for NHL, or an out-patient transplant process, why not.

Along those lines, and as I mentioned previously, for those of you in Southern California willing to donate blood, please contact the City of Hope. For those of you outside Southern California, while I would not ask you to come to the LA area just to donate on my behalf, please consider donating to your local Red Cross. Whole blood and platelets are in constant need and while not directly helping me, donating can help others. I gave blood on a regular basis for the last thirteen years but now having (and about to be able to say "had cancer"), I am no longer eligible to donate any blood product. So my blood/platelet needs in the future are dependent on the generosity of others.

With that, the sun is coming up, I'm already vertical (thanks Shiloh for the "early start") and it is a good day. I hope yours is as well. Thanks for continuing to care.

March 31ˢᵗ A.M.

March 31, 2014

The day is finally upon me. After the set back of the bacterial pneumonia, the 4 A.M. antibiotic infusions, numerous CT and PET scans (with another this morning), blood draws, chemo cycles, a whole host of medication(s) to take daily and whatever else could be hoisted upon me, the time has come to say good-bye to my cancer.

Transplant day is eight days away. Seven days of chemo treatments await me after today and then on April 8ᵗʰ, the harvested stem cells will be "transplanted" or returned to me and my immune system will start anew.

So I will head back to the City of Hope in a couple of hours to finish what was started late last summer. Whatever fear I have of the upcoming days is met by the prospect of being cancer free, an upcoming grandchild and the joy of living.

Please remember that Autumn and our girls are going through this with me and though they haven't gotten the chemo drugs, they have shared the ups and downs of this fight I've been fighting. I've been told many times the fight can be harder on the caregiver(s) than on the patient. My strength is in no small part a result of their strengths, caring and support. I shudder to think what this would have been like without their love.

I will probably be a bit quiet on the posting front until I get through the days of chemo. Please know that everyone who has reached out over these past almost eight months has had a hand in helping me get to today. I've received virtual HUGS (remember that stands for Hope, Understanding, Giving and Support), e-mails, phone calls, cards, letters, a few "care packages" and in some cases a visits to our home.

Geoff Berman

I've even heard that some of you are donating blood wherever you may be, something that was not otherwise in your regular routine. All of these have made my journey so far that much easier to get through.

The sun will be up soon (here at least) and I'm vertical. It will be a good day. There may be some tough days ahead, but they will all be "good" days when this process is over and I get to go home. Thanks for continuing to care.

March 31ˢᵗ P.M.

March 31, 2014

Welcome to the Hotel California dba City of Hope. I can now officially report that the results of today's PET scan have shown that the tumor and lung lesion are GONE!!!!! Remission is a good thing. I have checked in to hospital and will start the final ass-kicking tomorrow!!!! Let the transplant begin in earnest. The next few weeks will be filled with challenges but I will get through them all and put this in the rear view mirror.

To all, may I say that this journey, while not completely over, is in the final stretch. Again, I cannot begin to thank all of you enough for the support in words, calls, etc. for not just me but for all of us. This journey is definitely a family endeavor.

The sun is still up, I'm still vertical and it is a good day.

April Fools Day late afternoon

April 1, 2014

Don't get spoiled. No, I still may not post on a daily basis (no April Fools joke there).

I eased into the chemo process with a whole cast of folks stopping by, including the nutritionist, physical therapist, occupational therapist, social worker, case manager and I'm probably missing one or two. Got a shower, walked a mile with Mr. Pole, whose conversational skills haven't improved since I was last here; still nothing but beeping for attention and then a four hour chemo. Slept through almost all of it and then took another mile walk. Next is something for dinner so as not to be yelled at (the low bacteria diet is now in progress).

Day one will slow down after the shift change, as will I.

Thanks to everyone for the congratulatory words and calls after yesterday's news. They and everyone who takes a moment to think about Autumn, the girls, and me mean a great deal. We will not forget your love and caring.

The sun is out, I've been vertical and it's a good day.

April 7ᵗʰ P.M.

April 7, 2014

The seven days of chemo treatments are now behind me. I can't tell you if I'm worse for wear or not but I have no desire to run a 5K let alone a marathon. I did manage a two-mile walk this morning before the final chemo treatment. The transplanting of my harvested stem cells will take place tomorrow. Once I hit bottom, the rebuilding process will begin and then ultimately I will get to leave and go home.

Thank you for your continued thoughts, prayers and good wishes. They have helped as I work through this process to being cancer free. The sun is out, I'm (sort of) upright and it is a good day. More as I get closer to going home.

April 8th P.M.

April 8, 2014

A wonderful day all around as my stem cell transplant was done this morning and my road to full recovery continues. To top it off, Autumn and I became grandparents today as Arielle and Ryan brought Grey Louis Whitacre into the world this afternoon. How neat is that to share a birthday with your grandson.

The sun is up, I've been vertical and it is a very good day.

April 11th -Transplant Update

April 11, 2014

The news on the transplant front is that I am doing just what the doctors want - meaning I'm normal. Okay, for those of you who want to laugh, feel free, I will get even some other time. But seriously, in this case normal is good. I have been following the textbook apparently "by the book", which the doctors like. If they like it, I like it. My counts dropped overnight and I am now landlocked in my room. This was to be expected, though being limited to the smaller space does take a little getting used to.

I will start getting Neupogen again on Sunday, though this time by infusion rather than injection (yeah, I think). Once the counts come back up, to whatever the doctors call "normal", then I will be eligible to leave the hospital and go home. I don't expect that to take place for another week to ten days.

On the grandson front, he is doing well despite being a few weeks early. Mom and dad are dealing with everything very well and have had good conversations with Grey's doctors as well as both Autumn and me.

Assuming Grey continues to progress as he has so far, he should be home before the weekend is over. It is truly amazing to watch how our children's lives change when they find a loving spouse and start a family. Coupled with my getting past my cancer, this week brings a whole new meaning to "life".

The sun is up, I'm vertical (no I am not lying in my hospital bed all day thank you) and it is a good day. Thanks for continuing to follow this and care about us all.

April 14th - Update

April 14, 2014

The news from the front is slow and steady. My counts remain where expected, meaning I'm still tied to my room for now. Neupogen infusions began yesterday so as to aid the return to normalcy of the white blood cell counts. I continue to deal with the affects of the week's worth of chemo and even there, I appear to be normal. Some of those affects I could certainly do without (nausea and diarrhea) but then I'm not THAT special now no matter what I want to believe.

Today begins week three in the hospital. I am still coming to grips with the idea that this life saving process takes upwards of a month, but then again the alternatives don't compare well at all. So I take it one thing at a time, one procedure at a time and don't look too far forward to whenever the end date of my stay may be upon me.

All continues to go well on the grandson front as the Whitacre family adjusts to its new member and routine. Dad and son took a walk yesterday joining those in their neighborhood who walk the streets with little ones in tow or in stroller. They have all taken to it well.

We have all come so far in a relatively short period of time and I do look forward to my next steps in my progression to a return of good health and being cancer free.

The sun is up, I'm relatively vertical and it is a good day.

April 18th -Transplant plus ten

April 18, 2014

The current phrase to describe the routine in the hospital is "boring", as in humdrum, routine, not exciting and nothing extraordinary. More importantly it means that I am continuing to progress post transplant just as the doctors want, no emergencies, nothing requiring immediate attention, etc. Boring, and I'm okay with that.

My white blood cell count has finally started to regain some health as I'm now 0.3 today (hey, don't laugh as I was less than 0.1 for a few days there). Still get regular infusions of whole blood and platelets but I'm told nothing the doctors aren't expecting. As the white blood cell count rises, my grumpy stomach and diarrhea will begin to subside and then it will be get me back on something a kin to a regular diet.

The best news is that if things continue boring and progressing, there is a good chance I could be released from the hospital next week. I'd say it is because I was on good behavior, or that the staff was finally tired of me, but more realistically the transplant worked as it was supposed to and then I will be able to say I'm finally truly cancer free. Not saying that YET as I'm still in the hospital, but I'm a lot closer to saying that than for a long, long time.

Otherwise, the grandson front goes well, with Grey eating, sleeping, having hiccups and all the things newborns get to do. Mother and dad are handling everything comfortably to date and a routine around their house seems to be getting established. More this grandpa can't ask for.

With that, the sun is up, I've been vertical and it's a good day. I hope yours is as well.

April 25th

April 25, 2014

There is no news on the going home front as I somehow managed to find a virus wandering the halls looking for a home. Being the congenial host that I am I apparently opened my arms and welcomed it in. Silly (or stupid) me as the case may be. So two nights of fevers and a morning of a super grumpy stomach and I got to look behind door number three - an additional three nights stay at the Hotel California.

In the month that I have been resident here I have managed to become friendly with so much of the wonderful staff. Today they gave me an early department serenade, COH Hawaiian style. The staff had mustaches on their masks to make my lost mustache feel so much better. Thanks to Nicole for organizing this for me. It really helped with the still to be send off.

So until next week, the sun is up, I'm vertical (reasonably speaking)". It's a good day.

April 29th A.M.

April 29, 2014

After 29 days in the hospital, 58 nurse shift changes, 58 sets of PCA's (Patient Care Assistants), too many doctors to count, physical therapists, recreational therapists, clinical psychologists and social workers, more CT scans, chest x-rays and assorted other things, I AM FINALLY HOME!

According to the doctors, I was actually a pretty "boring" patient. Boring in that the transplant went pretty much according to the textbook. Believe me, I'm not complaining. The only "set back" if you will was I managed to find a virus last week that was basically the stomach/intestinal flu. So just about the time I started feeling better, up popped nausea, vomiting, diarrhea (again) and feeling generally *crappy* (that is not a medical term by the way). But all's well that end's well and it is good to be home.

It will take a while for the hospital sleep pattern to be erased (last night I woke up every two hours - no surprise). The girls looked at me when I came through the door and basically said, "Oh, you deemed us worthy of returning - about time". And then they ignored me until early this morning. Nice to have things sort of back to normal.

Now begins the process of rebuilding my strength and I have no doubt that that will be a slow process. I was pretty much thrashed physically over the last month so there is much to do to feel more normal, but after the transplant process, that should be a joy comparatively speaking. I've said this many times, but getting through this would not have been anywhere as easy without the love and support of Autumn, my family and friends. The tough days were made easier and the easy days that much better with the outpouring of support I have gotten. I owe all of you a huge debt of gratitude.

The sun is up (and quite warm as a matter of fact though I am not ready for the outside world quite yet), I'm definitely vertical. It is a very good day.

May 2nd A.M. 206+

May 2, 2014

The first follow up with the doctors at the City of Hope was yesterday and all is going as well as could be hoped. My white blood cell count is up over 3,000 (the low end or normal but normal), platelets are at 197, kidneys and liver are working as they should and the bone marrow is working. The doctor is happy and we are happy. I will have another PET scan at the end of the month to insure there is no more cancer and determine the need, if any, for radiation. I don't plan on worrying about that unless there is a need. Frankly, at this point it is good to hear that the road to recovery has begun, as the doctor(s) want and that the first trip back did not end up with a re-admission to the hospital.

Tomorrow I get the privilege of meeting my grandson for the first time - something I'm very much looking forward to. Strange to be a grandfather but I'm getting used to it, happily. Mom and dad continue to adjust to their son and their girls (cats) are adjusting to having a new living thing taking time from them - they'll get use to it. No sleeping in the crib with Grey however. Selene may be disappointed with the concept - Sammy probably not so much.

I'm adjusting to being back home slowly but happily. The sleep pattern remains a bit close to the hospital pattern but that will change with time. No sleeping pills for now thank you. Autumn and I had out first meal out last night when we got home from the doctor visit and it was nice to be "out", even if my eating remains a bit small and controlled. No heavy foods yet thank you. But I'm eating three meals a day and my system is slowly returning to the concept of real food versus TPN nutrition. I need to rebuild my leg strength and stability (of course losing 12 pounds while in the hospital might have something to do with that) but that will come with time.

The sun is up, I'm vertical and it is a good day. Thanks to everyone for their continued good thoughts and prayers - they are all loved and appreciated.

May 4th A.M. 206+

May 4, 2014

I got the joy of meeting my grandson for the first time yesterday on what was to have been his planned birthday. It's a very neat feeling holding our grandson at home having now been home close to a week. No I did not volunteer to change a diaper. I'll leave that to the parents' thank you. I'll let you decide which of the skinny folks is Grey and which is me. Autumn and I had a great time with Arielle, Ryan and Grey and are so appreciative of their taking the time to come out to our house to share the joy.

I am settling into the routine of being home again, slowly, but settling in. My strength is coming back a bit at a time and while my weight remains down, I've gained about a half a pound over the course of the last couple of days. Slow and steady wins this particular journey. It's been pretty windy here so I have not ventured outside much as I just don't need to risk wind born "things" attacking me. Frankly, I'm in no rush to try to be back to normal - that will and is taking time and I'd rather do this right this time than two or three times down the road. The proof is that I am slowly getting back to a bit more normal sleep pattern - but it's a ten hour sleep. So if I need the rest time, so be it. Otherwise, its one-hour at a time, one day at a time as the recovery process continues.

The sun is up, I'm vertical and it's a good day.

May 9th P.M.

May 9, 2014

The routine of recuperating is becoming more and more defined and it feels good to see improvement on a fairly regular basis. I certainly won't claim to be anywhere near ready for prime time, but each day that is better than the last brings me just a bit closer to feeling like my pre-cancer self. Let me not fool anyone, myself included. This remains a long, slow and tough road. Not every day is a feel good day but fortunately those do seem to be spaced out a bit. My appetite remains a bit slow to return, but I am eating three meals a day. Not necessarily big meals but still, three meals a day.

I continue to sleep more than ever before which obviously is symptomatic of how much I have to recover from the transplant that is now over a month old. Today Autumn and I went out and ran (well walked) errands around the Desert and I was able to make it out and about for a little over four hours. The couch is again my friend post errands, but that is okay.

We are having some work done on our house next week (something we had hoped would be done while I was in the hospital) and I will spend the time the house is in flux with Arielle, Ryan and Grey as there is no way for me to be around sawdust and wood glue. I'm looking forward to spending time with all the Whitacre's even though I won't be able to be home to help with supervising the work. Next week is also the next follow up visit with the doctors at the City of Hope where I expect (or at least hope) that the reports will continue to be positive.

Thanks for continuing to follow my efforts to overcome my cancer. Here's to my mother this coming Mother's Day (she has already received her Mother's Day hedgehogs thank you), Autumn as the mother of our girls and Arielle as our newest Mother.

Beyond that, the sun is up, I'm vertical and it has been a good day and a few good days since my last post.

May 14ᵗʰ A.M.

May 14, 2014

Had another round of follow up testing and doctor visit yesterday at the City of Hope. I am happy to report that I continue to progress well post transplant, now 34 days ago. Blood counts remain in the normal range and my doctor continues to be pleased. If she is pleased, then Autumn and I are pleased.

I also had a 3.5 hour I.V. IG infusion. (I.V. IG stands for **Intravenous immunoglobulin**). **IV IG** contains the pooled, <u>polyvalent</u>, <u>IgG</u> antibodies extracted from the plasma of over one thousand blood donors and aids in the rebuilding of one's immune system or used as treatment acquired compromised immunity conditions (secondary immune deficiencies) featuring low antibody levels. That certainly applies to one having had a stem cell transplant like me. So if this is needed to help me fend off infection, then no issues from me going through the infusion. Of course having the first i.v. site crash within ten minutes leaving a nice bruise wasn't contemplated but this too will pass. So it looks like things continue to progress well. I will find out in two weeks the status of the tumor when I have my next PET scan.

Otherwise, my efforts to rebuild my strength continue, one day at a time. I'm looking forward to getting back to some of the activities from my pre-cancer days, but only as my strength allows.

The sun is up, I'm vertical and yes, it is a good day.

149

May 23ʳᵈ A.M.

May 23, 2014

Things have been pretty quiet, though I won't say each day revisits the prior one (no, its not Groundhog Day!). My strength level does seem to be improving, little by little. I'm still not ready for a 5k walk thank you, but the use of my cane is now much more sporadic. Sleep is still a high priority including naps, which do seem to arrive sometimes unannounced - and that's okay.

We had new floors installed in most of our house and with some new furniture in the family room, its almost like a new house. Even the cats have gotten to where they seem to approve. Keeping the floors clean will be much easier (mostly for Autumn as I'm not allowed to do much when it comes to dirt, dust and the like).

The next progress report comes on the 28ᵗʰ, with more blood to be drawn and a PET scan. After that, we will have a better idea of what lies in store over the next month or so. In the meantime, Michelle is here for a visit and it is nice to see her more than once a year and as my travel remains restricted for a while, a good chance to hear first hand how things are going. Add a little work and some hugs, and I've got little to complain about.

Yes, the sun is up, I'm vertical and it is a good day.

Thank you for continuing to follow my travels through this cancer and recovery. May you have a happy Memorial Day Holiday weekend with family and/or friends.

Memorial Day

May 26, 2014

As we pause to remember those who fought to protect our freedom, let me take a moment to thank those who have worked to return me to good health, from my internist, the three sets of oncologists, the nursing staffs at the Desert Regional Medical Center's Comprehensive Cancer Center and the City of Hope and all the technicians, radiologists and other professionals that have given their time to help me through my fight with cancer. They are heroes in their own way, as much in many ways, as those who serve here and abroad. Yes, we stop and think about these professionals through the various charitable organizations we are asked to support and the stories of those around us fighting the same type of fight I've been through the many months, but they often are unsung heroes in our personal fights.

On a lighter note, the photo attached with this post shows what happens when one uses cheese wiz with a chiopet. Seriously, thanks to Miss Emily, long a neighbor and friend of our girls and ours, who now calls Madison, WI home. So a Cheese Head I am (at least for a moment) and until someone gives me a cheese grater head (I'm told Chicago Bears' fans wear these when playing the Packers). It's another way to keep one's head warm besides a wool cap!

Michelle is now winging her way back to Michigan after a week's visit. She got to meet her nephew and spend most of the week here with us in the Desert. The volume here is back to our "normal", but it is nice to see her progress to being a mature woman. And does she enjoy Crossfit. We always knew she had to have some athletic endeavor to keep her energized and it appears Crossfit is it.

On this Memorial Day, the sun is up, I'm vertical and it is a good day. Please take a moment to remember those who have served us, be it in the military, or a medical professional who has made a close friend or relative's life a bit easier.

May 30th A.M. Finally, REMISSION

May 30, 2014

After nine and a half months, nine chemo cycles plus the week of chemo as part of the stem cell transplant, four PET scans, numerous CT scans, two bone marrow aspirations and other forms of testing too numerous to count (or remember), my doctor told us on Wednesday that I was now cancer free and in remission. It has been a long and trying road, as you who have been reading these posts understand. But coming out the other side healthy and free of this unwanted resident is worth the fight. There is a chance that the doctors will want me to undergo radiation therapy to insure that any remnant tumor cells are completely eradicated, but with the tumor's location being so close to the hip/pelvic bone and where the body generates bone marrow, they may decide it is not necessary. I'm patiently waiting to hear their decision.

There is still much for me to do to be ready to return to some facsimile of life before cancer. I am back on the Bactrim, this time as a preventative measure to avoid a reoccurrence of the bacterial infection that slowed the transplant process early this year and will likely be on that antibiotic for at least 90-120 days. One of the side-effects of Bactrim is to suppress white blood cells so it remains important that I continue the recovery process carefully choosing when and where I go in public, as well as staying away from those with fevers, colds, etc. Nothing personal, just I don't need to let others impact my recovery if I know of their illness in advance. But at least at this point, both Autumn and I can take a deep breath and begin relaxing as hopefully the worst for me is behind us.

Lest there be any doubt, the rigors of fighting cancer, or any disease, is as tough on the primary caregiver as it is on the patient. I have been a first hand witness to this now and Autumn has earned a break. We made a deal when my tumor was discovered last August that when I was in remission and able to fend for myself (more than throughout the treatment process), she would get a week of rest, relaxation and de-stressing at Canyon Ranch in Tucson. She made her reservation for a few weeks from now and is already looking forward to the trip. And I'm glad to be well so she can take a break from the stress of treatment and recovery and have some "just for her time". She's earned it and then some.

So while my traversing through the rigors of cancer is not yet finished, the toughest part is in the rear view mirror. Many thanks to everyone who has helped us, who have read these posts, called, e-mailed, come by - they have all helped me get to today. I'm not done posting as that will continue until I'm allowed back into the working world in-person in a couple of months and it will hopefully mark the end of the fight (symbolically if nothing else). There will be years of follow up testing and check ups, but that is normal for any cancer survivor and know I'm pleased to be counted as one of the survivors.

The sun is up and I'm vertical. The last few days have been very good days, as will today.

June 2nd

June 2, 2014

With remission now a firmly established part of my life going forward (and still no word as to the need for radiation), I have embarked on getting stronger so that my return to the more normal working world will be easier. I started a walking program a little over a week ago and a minimum of a one-mile walk is now part of the daily routine. The first such mile took 25 minutes and led to an hour-long nap (gee, what a surprise).

Yesterday and today I dropped the time and upped the pace to a 21-minute mile (and NO nap yesterday - today is too soon to tell). Once I get the time under 20 minutes, then I will start adding additional laps around the indoor track until I can get to three miles in an hour. Lest anyone think the transplant process and the chemo before it scrambled my brains (I know, very funny), with temperatures in the Desert already in the upper 90's to 105, I am using the indoor track for these walks - I am not walking outside in the heat.

I've also been cleared to return to the pool, though after dusk as I can't take the daytime sun on my skin to that extent without risking skin cancer - no thanks. I expect to walk a bit and use the Jacuzzi soon if for no reason other than I now can.

I am also reminded that my outcome is one not everyone achieves. A friend has kept me informed of someone going through Stage IV breast cancer that has moved into her liver. The prognosis isn't good and so far, the chemotherapy and other protocols have failed to return her to good health. A bright person much younger than me and without something close to divine intervention, she will be one who doesn't get to share the exhilaration of surviving. Forget what is or isn't fair. It is hard to know so many others struggle to fight their particular cancer without success and cure.

So take a moment please and think positive thoughts for this lady and that for most of us, good health is taken for granted. The sun is up, I'm vertical and for me, it is a good day.

June 8th

June 8, 2014

Its now sixty days since the transplant and so far, so good. I am reminded that my good fortune is just that, good fortune. Not everyone who goes through this, or any other cancer treatment, sees the positives I have so far. For that, I am so grateful.

We had a weekend visit from Arielle, Ryan and Grey this weekend and that adds to the fun of our daily routines. Probably a bit tougher on Grey's parents that the grandparents, but we did "baby sit" yesterday while Arielle and Ryan treated themselves to a few hours of massages and pampering. Grey, as were his grandparents, was well behaved.

Next up is the continuation of the rest and rebuilding of strength. I continue to walk or do something every day. I do see progress, little by little. I can't say time is flying by, but a week from now it will be ten months from discovery to remission/recovery. Wow.

More than that, the sun is up and I'm definitely vertical. It is a good day.

Father's Day 2014 ▓▓▓▓▓▓▓▓▓▓▓▓▓▓▓▓▓▓▓▓

June 15, 2014

A bright and warm Father's Day morning; may the day bring joy to all, whether Father's, Mother's, sons or daughters.

I continue to be reminded of just how fortunate I am having made it through my treatment for cancer and gotten to remission. It seems that those I learn of that have their own fights with cancer haven't been so lucky as two people I recently came in contact with through friends and family lost their respective battles in the last week.

One, a 38-year-old mother of a 16 month old and wife, the other a young (30) father and husband. Their passing makes me pause to appreciate even more the opportunity I have to be a survivor. No doubt as people read this and other postings, you too know somebody fighting cancer of some type - please remember they too need all the love and support that you and others can share. It makes the fight that much easier, not that the fight is ever easy and sadly, not always successful.

I continue to work on getting stronger and being able to move back into a more normal working world. My weight seems to have stabilized around 205, almost 30 pounds from where I was in May 2013 and 15 pounds down from the date of my first chemo (R-CHOP) treatment. I haven't tried on any of my suits yet, but if they are like the rest of my clothes, there is probably room for an extra part of me or two in there. I am in no hurry to return to the 230's either. I can also report the mustache is coming around after being thrashed by the last of the pre-transplant chemo drugs (the nasty Melphalan). It's not back to its pre-cancer days, but getting there.

My next follow up visit to the doctors at the City of Hope is in ten days, so for now, the daily routine remains relatively static. Assuming I continue this way, airplane travel becomes legal for me again in mid-August and a work conference and a few days of Hawaiian breezes await Autumn and me. We both are looking forward to the trip.

So yes, the sun is up and I'm vertical. It is a good day.

June 21ˢᵗ A.M.

June 21, 2014

Welcome to Summer. As if on cue, the Desert has gotten "hot" with temperatures not expected to be below 108 for at least a week and low temps around 90. Its no wonder snow birds migrate north in the Spring and return here in the late Fall. But I'm not complaining as I get to experience another season and frankly that for me is more important. So a little heat will be tolerated.

My next follow up visit is next week and I am looking forward to a continued good report from the doctors. This trip includes a once over by my infectious disease doctor checking that the nocardia hasn't returned. After this visit I may get to go another month without a check up, meaning that I continue to do well post transplant. That's the goal anyway. Assuming that to be the case, I will be closer to returning to the office, even if on a limited basis. Now going into the eleventh month of this journey (from diagnosis at least) even that is a step that means I am doing well and moving forward. I'll take it. I'm still dealing with the neuropathy in my feet but it doesn't stop me from walking and getting some exercise. It will be nice when that goes away. I've even gotten back on the Wii for some Wii Fit workouts. Scary.

This past Father's Day Autumn and I walked the Cabazon outlet mall for a change of pace. On our way home we stopped by the Palm Springs Airport for a glimpse of Air Force One while the President was "vacationing" in town. It's a beautiful sight to behold (reasonably up close) and a symbol of the freedoms that we enjoy being a citizen of the US. We saw the new Jersey Boys movie yesterday afternoon. As with the Broadway show, the music is wonderful and the story is well told (to an even greater extent than the play). We were surprised by the large audience at an afternoon matinee on opening day but happy to be able to join in the fun. Autumn and I got to see Frankie Valli perform a couple of years ago and while the voice is a tad bit ragged now, he still sounds darn close to when he and the Four Seasons broke into the music scene in the 1960's.

May the summer months bring joy to all, a respite from the cold of winter and the cool Spring, with barbeques, good friends and good times. There is enough suffering from dealing with cancer and other diseases not to smile as the sun warms the sky and hopefully our hearts. And yes, the first sunrise of summer finds me vertical thankfully and it is a good day.

June 26th P.M.

June 26, 2014

Another visit to the City of Hope has come and gone and the news to report continues to be good. All my blood work came in at levels the doctor felt was more than acceptable, at least for now. The transplant was 79 days ago and the 90-day milestone is fast upon me. So far, so good. I also saw the infectious disease doctor who dealt with the nocardia infection in my lung and that too remains quiet and for all intents and purposes gone. I remain on the two antibiotics for precautionary reasons and likely will be for another ninety days.

I still need to get stronger as the effort to drive to/from the City of Hope, all the testing and poking, leave me pretty worn out. I am still not ready to drive to the office for a few days so I continue to work from home and contribute any way I can. The good news is that if things continue this way, Hawaii (conference and "vacation") is still a go. I will have a check up just before we are to leave in August for the final "okay".

Beyond that, the summer heat has made our routine a bit less spur of the moment going out (its only 100 today versus 108 yesterday) and next week could be as high as 114. The heat saps my strength as much as exercise, but I take it as another tool to get me stronger.

Autumn heads out soon for her week of R&R after eighteen months of dealing first with her mother's cancer and ultimate passing and then my cancer fight. She's earned this respite. The cats and I will be fine - we all promised Autumn we would behave.

The sun has been up and I've been vertical - it is a good day.

July 1st

July 1, 2014

Welcome to July and the blast furnace called the Desert. It is a toasty 108 this afternoon and expected to top out at 114 tomorrow. For me, it means staying indoors and not letting myself get too hot. Its still tough enough to get my strength back as it is to be trying to combat the outdoors. These lyrics resonate with me as what the entirety of the cancer process has been like:

> When there is no place safe and no safe place to put my head, When you feel the world shake from the words that are said, And I'm calling all angels, I'm calling all you angels"

And all you Angels came to support me in my time of need and Autumn and I are and will be forever grateful. I give thanks every day that I am through the lion's share of the process and in remission now. I continue to look forward to resuming a more normal schedule soon, though soon may be a few weeks away still.

The sun has been up, I'm vertical, and yes, it's been a good day.

July 8th - Transplant plus 90

July 8, 2014

It's been ninety days since my stem cell transplant and the birth of Grey Whitacre, our grandson (easy to remember that isn't it when they are on the same day). I'm feeling good (not quite great, but certainly good). The hold back is that my strength is taking longer to come back to where I would like it than I might have hoped, but with what I've been through, I shouldn't and am not that surprised. Not even disappointed.

I picked up my bowling ball yesterday for the first time really since last July. It took a bit to get the steps to where I was comfortable, but I had a very decent series for three games (168-215-192=575). Surprised me that's for sure. Autumn was a bit surprised too. Add a thirty-minute walk in the morning and I slept pretty well last night.

Autumn had a great time at Canyon Ranch and came back refreshed and ready for the next challenge that may be before us (whatever that may be). She took full advantage of the variety of things offered at the facility, including massages, cooking demonstrations, group discussions, etc. She had a full schedule for a week and I was glad that I am now in a position that she could have the week away without worrying about me.

More than that there really isn't. No, my routine is not "boring", in part because it varies daily, but there is time for exercise, time for whatever work needs attention, time to read, rest and be with friends. I had neighbors make sure I did not go hungry (hardly likely) while Autumn was away and while I did not gain any weight (I'm currently at 207) while she was gone, I did not lose any either. However, I can report that my mustache is almost back to the pre-chemo fullness. Much better than the non-mustache look I must say.

Arielle and Ryan celebrated their second wedding anniversary yesterday. Once again, time flies. It is nice to see them grow in their relationship, now with Grey as a part of their family.

Thanks for continuing to follow these posts, as I get closer to the return to a more normal lifestyle. The sun is up (yes, it is still warm - okay HOT - here in the Desert but we knew that going in), I'm vertical (we walked again early this morning about two miles) so it is a good day.

July 15th - Another Birthday

July 15, 2014

A date on the calendar is just that, a date or day, each to be lived to its fullest. I've written before about perspective and how dealing with cancer changes that for the patient, the caregiver and family and friends. Some dates mean just a bit more. For me, August 21st will always mean the realization that something was terribly wrong to the point my internist told me the "test results aren't good". No way to ever forget that. Just like our daughters' birthdays, our wedding anniversary and other key dates, that date will always have special meaning. So will April 8th, when our grandson was born and I had my stem cell transplant. Coincidence or not, a special bond with Grey because of that date on the calendar.

Today is another special day. Yes, it is my birthday (no applause necessary now :-)) but it the first such celebration after becoming cancer free. So in many ways, it is my 61st and 1st birthdays wrapped into one. I hope it will be the first of many. Those of you who have read these musings for now almost a year know what a long and in many ways trying road this has been. Let's not sugar coat it - it was harder than anything I could have imagined. Physically, emotionally and just about any way you can think of. But with everyone's HUGS (remember, that stands for Hope, Understanding, Giving and Support) in so many ways, I have made it to remission and soon, to be able to begin my slow return to the working world "*in person*".

Hawaii, with both an ABI conference and some down time in Kauai is now less than a month away, subject to passing two more post treatment follow-up testing/doctor visits. I expect nothing less than passing grades both times. No, my strength is not yet where I would like it to be but I am more realistic than ever. This process beat the living s - - - out of me and it's taking longer than I ever imagined it would to be close to the old normal. Maybe the new normal is less strong, but I'm not going to let that stop me.

So today is a day of celebrating. Dinner out at a steak house no less - I'm finally ready for that steak I passed on for so many months due to the chemo cycles and their after effects, and a get together with some friends here in our community tomorrow night after our weekly bocce game. We had dinner with Arielle, Ryan and Grey last Saturday to celebrate as well, so I get to bask in the sunlight of this milestone and enjoy every minute of it.

Then, it will be back at the process of recovery, looking forward and being able to say thank you to so many for so much, in person, one of these days.

The sun is up, I'm vertical and today is and will be a very good day.

July 15th - Evening

July 15, 2014

Just to complete the day, dinner and the STEAK were marvelous. Thank you Morton's for a truly special evening. And no, I did not share the steak - Autumn had her own! We did share the mashed potatoes and spinach and mushrooms (sorry, we like mushrooms). A wonderful day all around. Thanks to everyone for being a part of it.

The sun is setting, I'm still vertical (barely for the day at least) and it has been a great day.

July 23rd A.M.

July 23, 2014

Another post transplant follow up yesterday with the results being very good and having Dr. Nademanee very pleased. We remain of the mindset that if she is happy, so are we (that would be Autumn and me). If I get the same results on August 11th, then our trip to Hawaii is on for sure. No reason to think there will be any change between now and then.

This past weekend I got the chance to go to my Mom's house in Oceanside for the first time since the tumor was discovered. Arielle, Ryan and Grey joined us for a four-generation get together and picture session. Michelle was back in Michigan, enjoying a visit from her boyfriend, but there in spirit. Lunch was the last of my birthday celebrations. It was a good feeling to be able to see my Mom in her home versus making her come to me. No doubt it won't be another year before I get down there again.

Strength and reserves remain much less than I would like so that continues to be my focus over the coming weeks. Two days of attending a meeting by Skype, plus the trip to the City of Hope and back, and the testing, left me more than a little tired. Before cancer, six - to -seven hours sleep was a good night's sleep; last night was ten hours. I'll get there.

I'm still dealing with the effects of the neuropathy that showed up during the R-CHOP cycles. Nothing that can't be dealt with, but the sensation through my feet is constant and often annoying (livable compared to cancer, but still annoying). The neuropathy also affects balance every now and then (not so fun when one stands up and you feel a bit wobbly) and a couple of other things. I also am going to have my eyes checked as the steroids given with the chemo cycles can cause cataracts. But none of these things are debilitating versus trying to beat cancer. Just hurdles to happily overcome.

A high pressure bubble is moving over the Southwest with a heat advisory beginning today through Friday, with high temps as much as 117. Needless to say, don't expect us to be active with outside activities. Otherwise, yes, the sun is up, I'm vertical and it will be a good day.

July 26th Afternoon

July 27, 2014

Little change to report, which is a good thing. What strikes me though is just how often cancer strikes near us. Until it strikes in our home or immediate business or personal family, we almost become immune to yet another cancer victim and their plight. Try being 5 years old with neuroblastoma and needing surgery to have a chance at life. That is the current situation for Desi Cechin.

See http://www.desertsun.com/story/news/local/2014/07/23/desi-cechin-cancer-surgery-paid/13080809/ for an article about her fight. Her oncologist is the same doctor that took care of me through my chemo treatments, Elber Camacho, MD, Medical Director of the Desert Regional Medical Center Comprehensive Cancer Center. He is what the article says, a caring doctor who does whatever he can for his patients. Period.

I probably would have not given a story about a 5 year old with cancer much thought a year ago. Now, the hurt she is suffering, the chemo and radiation treatments (the latter I fortunately avoided) and the upcoming surgery are hard to ignore. I've been there, done my share of that. And her parents can't be having any fun either. Just ask Autumn.

This is not to say that Desi, or anyone else is more special than others. It does however go to show just how far reaching cancer is in our lives. Some day, may the researchers find cures for the common cancers and then the more difficult ones, so that cancer patients don't have to experience the trauma of the diagnosis and treatment. I've made it through mine yes, but I have been forever changed in this regard - cancer is now a part of my life (and the family) and others who face the diagnosis need all the love and support we can give them. Whether its a hug, taking them a meal, financial support to a fundraising activity, whatever, please think twice the next time you have the opportunity to help others with cancer. They, like me, no doubt will appreciate it. (Enough for my soapbox.)

The sun is up and I'm vertical. It is a good day. Thanks for continuing to read these musings.

July 27th A.M.

July 28, 2014

As a follow up to yesterday's post (okay, quoting my friend Peter Baccaro, my soap box) in speaking with Michelle yesterday she told me about the work Kaitlin Sandeno (for those of you not in the swimming world, a US Olympian swimmer from El Toro, CA) is doing for the Jessie Rees Foundation, as its national spokesperson. If you don't know Jessie's story, it is one of true caring and love, as despite being diagnosed with cancer in the brain, she wanted to help other children. She created what became the *Joy Jar*, jars filled with things that make a child smile. Today over eighty thousand Joy Jars have been distributed to children fighting cancer across the country through her foundation. Jessie lost her fight with cancer quickly, but her spirit lives on through her foundation and the caring of others. Her motto is a take off on that of Jim Valvano (whom I mentioned months ago), its "Never Ever Give Up" (NEGU). For more on this inspirational story go to www. negu.org. Much like Steve Gleason, the former football player fighting ALS and his "No White Flags" (www.teamgleason.org), the message is simple, don't give in, don't give up and live each day to its fullest.

Again, there are so many people touched by cancer and too many children having to fight this fight. Any means of support of any of the hundreds of organizations that work to make patients' lives and their families that much easier, or by giving blood (something I used to do every 60 days or so for almost fifteen years but am prohibited from doing ever again because of my cancer and treatment) or platelets, or whatever makes you happy, please take a moment to do so. No, we can't do everything but consider it a way to pay it forward.

As for Autumn and me, and I know Michelle and Arielle and Ryan, finding a way to support some organization dealing with cancer and its victims (I do hate that word but it is appropriate here) will be a part of our lives from now on. We won't ignore the plight of others as readily as we did before; we won't give to every cause for we don't have those types of resources. Think about joining in a 5k-walk/run or bake sale or whatever you may hear about. A couple of hours will leave you feeling wonderful about giving and sharing. But having been there and with the help of so many friends with their moral support, I get to be a lucky one who right now is a survivor.

So for me, today is another day where the sun is up, I'm vertical and it is a good day. I hope it is for you too.

August 2nd A.M.

August 2, 2014

We enter August, the month my tumor was finally uncovered, meaning its almost been a year since my internist's call with "the (test) results are not good". Boy what a year it's been. As regular followers of this post know, I've had my share of ups and downs, set backs and most importantly, success in treating my cancer. I talked with the transplant coordinator at my insurance carrier recently and she too remarked how well I am doing, especially compared to many others under her watch. I can't tell you why, but I'm not refusing. I just continue to go about things one day at a time.

Autumn and I are going to a concert tonight, the first we have ventured to attend since the transplant. Figuring that at this point I should be better able to handle a bit of a crowd, we will head off for the evening to hear Daughtry perform.

I noted a few posts ago that I finally got to my Mom's house and that Arielle, Ryan and Grey were there as well. I've attached and posted this photograph that Ryan took of the four generations of Berman's/Whitacre's. It was a special day and a joy to share young Mr. Grey with his great grandmother again. I'm the short bald guy. (I know, ah da!)

While dealing with the family front, Michelle is now in the process of moving back to Southern California, marking the end of her six year sojourn to the Eastern time zone (granted four years were for college at Rutgers but that still counts). She is looking forward to moving to the Desert and being closer to Mom and Dad, her sister, Ryan and of course Grey. Being closer to grandma too doesn't hurt. Our family get togethers will be a bit bigger from here on out.

Next up for me is the pre-Hawaii blood test and doctor visit (dare I say final approval to fly) and a follow up visit with a new ophthalmologist, as I've been having (not so much) fun with a large floater that is being watched closely so as to not have it create any problems with the retina in the affected eye. Just another thing to deal with. So until then, its the daily routine as usual.

Thanks for continuing to follow my musings. The sun is up, I'm vertical and it is a good day. I hope it is for you as well.

August 11th P.M.
"Hello World, how've you been, well its good to see you again"

August 11, 2014

Best news of a wonderful day. My travel restriction has been officially lifted! Today's blood work and doctor visit continue to show progress in my remission phase from my cancer and while my white blood cell count is down, that is attributable to the Bactrim (antibiotic) that I continue to take to prevent a reoccurrence of my bacterial infection from early this year. So Autumn and I will get to join our friends at the ABI Hawaiian Conference on Maui in two days and thereafter, enjoy a week in Princeville, Kauai with Arielle, Ryan and Grey. Having gotten the go ahead, I'm now excited. No doubt the "joys" of airplane travel will remind us in no time what the hurry up and wait aspect of travel is, but at least this time around, I'll manage without too much suffering.

With the Sun up, I'm definitely vertical and it has been a very good day.

Aloha.

August 13th A.M. Hawaii Bound

August 12, 2014

Today marks the beginning of this new adventure, returning to the friendly skies and the tropical breezes that mark the islands of Hawaii. It will be the first real travel I've had in almost a year. Physically there remain some risks as my white blood cell count remains low (see my prior post for that) and being with a couple hundred strangers on a plane for five plus hours will be new for this post transplant guy but not new in life. But like everything we get to deal with, an experience to embrace and enjoy.

I've noted in the past the work done by the City of Hope in the field of bone marrow and for me, stem cell transplants. One of the leading facilities of its kind in California and the nation, the City of Hope continues to develop new treatment therapies for these transplants. The newest innovation is outpatient transplants at the City of Hope's day hospital. It would not have worked for me as so far, only multiple myeloma patients are getting the outpatient procedure (and of course we don't live less than an hour from Duarte except by helicopter or tele-transport). But the news is exciting for those who face this regimen to cure their cancer. For more information about this new procedure, see http://breakthroughs.cityofhope.org/bone-marrow-transplant-outpatient. One of the doctors involved in setting up this process, Dr. Leslie Popplewell, was on the team under Doctor Nademanee, treating me.

So yes, cancer is now firmly a part of my life, with Autumn and the girls (and Ryan and Grey) and the work done by so many to find cures will remain a priority for me for the rest of my life. Not to the exclusion of other things or causes (including pet rescues - like our cats), but with a much more focused view than prior to August 2013.

I remain indebted to you for following these musings and me for they bring me the knowledge that I'm helping others beside myself. The sun will be up (yes, this is quite early for this post) and I'm vertical. It will be a good day.

August 14th A.M. HST

August 14, 2014

Aloha from Maui. Yes, after the clearance from the doctor(s) including my new ophthalmologist, Autumn and I made it across the Pacific yesterday to Maui and the start of eleven days of some conference time and then family time on Kauai. As much as we love our Desert home, it is nice to have a change of scenery. A very added plus is to reconnect with some of our ABI friends in person and many HUGS were exchanged last night.

The sounds of the waves and the wind are a pleasant reminder of the variety of experiences life provides us and a phrase my mother gave me years ago comes to mind. The earth has music for those who listen. Like everything else for me now, I treasure these new chances to experience the music of life and the friendship of those who have been so supportive this past year.

The sun is up, I'm vertical and it is a good day. Aloha.

August 18th A.M. HST

August 18, 2014

Aloha from Kauai. As the picture notes, the sun is (coming) up and I'm vertical already, in part due to the sounds of Grey playing early this morning with one of his play mats and toys. It's a bit hard to explain time zones to a four month old and for this purpose I'm a bit older than four months thank you. It's nice to be back at hour Hawaiian "home" and we are all looking forward to some relaxation along with the island breezes.

Maui was lovely, though Autumn and I prefer Kauai. More importantly, we got the chance to see so many of our ABI friends and express our gratitude for their love and support throughout this long year. That in and of itself made the Maui stay more than worthwhile.

So now it's family time, with some work thrown in as that does generally seem to happen when we get away. But with the sun up and being vertical, it is a good day. I hope yours is as well.

August 20th P.M. HST

August 20, 2014

Kauai is like home to us and it is good to see some of our friends at the resort and as with our ABI friends in Maui, be so welcomed back into the day-to-day world we have come to love. Our first few days have been filled with very little, some relaxation, a few naps, a Lappert's run for ice cream and a whole lot of little else. Sure, we sit out by the pool, but I'm under a canopy and have a rash guard on to protect me from the sun, plus my hat; add a towel to cover my legs as necessary so I don't get too much sun and I'm definitely behaving.

Grey has been a joy to have share this part of the trip. Oh yes, he has his moments and his "shark attacks" as Arielle and Ryan call them, but he gets lots of attention from everyone besides the family and he eats it up with a spoon, a giggle and a smile. Ham.

As evidenced by Arielle and Ryan modeling for tonight's evening shot, the sun has been up, I've been vertical and it has been a good day.

August 25th A.M.

August 25, 2014

The Hawaii stay is over and we have returned to the Desert, reasonably refreshed and having had a wonderful week with Arielle, Ryan and Grey (who did very well on the flight back to LA). So now its back to the routine here, though with some additional work to help Michelle as she relocates to Palm Desert two weeks from today.

It has now been over a year since my tumor was found and we began the process of diagnosing and then treatment(s). As those of you who have followed me over the course of the past year through these musings know, the year has been filled with highs, lows, ups and downs and everything in-between. As I hopefully get close to being able to return to the office, even on a limited basis, I will have to look at my suits as there is likely a need for some tailoring to address the lost weight - it could be worse.

The future looks bright, even if my routine of old is no longer. That's okay and I will learn a new routine. But the chance to get out into the working public and see our Kauai "home" has made the upcoming weeks all the easier to adjust to. I expect that the second year of my dealing with cancer will prove a bit less challenging than the first (though I am not complaining about the results mind you).

The sun is up and despite less than a full night's sleep (thank you Shiloh), I'm vertical. It is a good day.

August 29ᵗʰ P.M.

August 29, 2014

A quick note before the Labor Day Holiday weekend comes upon all of us. I weighed in this morning at 213, up seven pounds since coming home on April 28ᵗʰ from my stem cell transplant. I don't want to go up much more so exercise and diet (what I eat versus "dieting") will be keys in my future. Because I have begun traveling and now have a business trip on the near term horizon for a mediation, its time to dust off the suits and check for size. No surprise, the suit jackets are fine; the pants have a bit of alteration to be done to account for the lost "butt". The first two suit pants went to the tailor this morning - its better than buying new suits. Not sure how my neuropic feet will appreciate being in dress shoes after a year, but I will tackle that like everything else, one day at a time.

Arielle and Ryan took possession of their new house this past Tuesday and the renovations will begin in earnest over the weekend. Grey started daycare as Mom started her 2014-2015 teaching duties yesterday, just to make matters more "fun". I was able to see the new house before the demolition work begins as that dust and work are not in my health's best interests. I hate being selfish, its not in my nature, but I do have to be protective of my reborn immune system. The kids understand that I'm not staying away just because. Call it long distance moral support. Autumn is helping with more hands on things, though even that will be fairly limited in nature.

Michelle begins her journey of returning to Southern California in a week and her apartment awaits here in the Desert. It will be the first time in six years she will be close to "home", be it our home in the Desert or her sister/brother-in-law in the LA basin. I know she is looking forward to being back "home". We are looking forward to it too.

The Desert has had a furnace blast yesterday and today and we are back in the 110-114's. Probably one more September/October heat wave to endure but then we move back into the pleasant time of year (and the return of the snow birds). This cycle of living here is becoming familiar and comfortable.

Thanks for continuing to follow my journey. May the Holiday weekend bring you the chance for family and friends and a send off of Summer. As for me, yes, the sun is up, I'm vertical and it is a good day and will be a good weekend.

September 7th P.M.

September 7, 2014

Back from my second ABI Conference in just over three weeks (this time in Las Vegas) and it was so nice to renew friendships and to let people see I really am doing okay. Last night Autumn and I saw the Cirque Du Soleil Michael Jackson "One" show and unlike some of the other music anthologies, this was a spectacular program combining Michael Jackson's music and the acrobatics of Cirque Du Soleil without any significant storyline.

I found the following quote Michael Jackson to be prophetic and even if not directly intended for dealing with cancer, I think it still can apply:

> "In a world filled with hate, we must dare to hope.
> In a world filled with anger, we must still dare to comfort.
> In a world filled with despair, we must still dare to dream.
> And in a world filled with distrust, we must dare to believe."

Those of us whose lives are filled with fighting cancer, or supporting our loved ones as they fight on, must be positive and dare to dream and dare to believe we will get well. Giving in the despair and anger only serves to lessen the likelihood of survival and those negative thoughts need to remain outside our world.

On the family front, Michelle is now a day away from relocating here to the Desert. She and her cats are winding their way across the Midwest and at last report, were close to Interstate 15 in Utah. The Whitacre cold and cough(s) are getting better - so all is good. Tuesday is my next PET scan and the news of its results will be reported shortly thereafter.

The sun has been up, I have been vertical and it is a good day.

September 8ᵗʰ A.M.

September 8, 2014

For those of you hearing about the remnants of Norbert "dumping" rain on the Southwest (Phoenix primarily but including our area), the reports are true. This picture is from our backyard. The greenbelt doubles as a flood control channel. All of the water has gathered in the last 75 minutes. We are fine - just amazed at the level of rising water.

The sun is out (somewhere), I'm vertical and it is a god day.

September 9th P.M. ▨▨▨▨▨▨▨▨▨▨▨▨

— Sep 9, 2014 10:35pm

The results are in and the PET scan revealed no return of my cancer. My tumor site has some mass left, but it is not active at all. Five months post transplant and I remain cancer free. My white blood cell count was down a bit more but the doctor thinks it's directly related to the constant Bactrim doses I'm on to insure the nocardia does not return. My dosage was reduced today and I will be off both antibiotics at the end of the month.

I was also allowed to start going back to my LA office, which we did after the scan and doctor visit. Only a couple of days a week on weeks not traveling, but it's a step in the right direction. It was a bit strange walking into the office this afternoon for the first time to work in over a year. An ABI commission call tomorrow morning while Autumn sees the dentist and then back to the Desert we go, but it is a good change and Autumn will get a few days every now and then without me home.

The sun was shining brightly today, I most certainly was vertical (when not preparing for or in the scanner) and it has been a very good day.

September 10th A.M.

Sep 10, 2014 12:11pm

Well, it's been a long time but this morning the work clothes were put back on (for the first time in well over a year) as evidenced by the picture above. No it's not a selfie as Autumn was the photographer. Dress shoes are currently NOT my friend so it may be tennis shoes for a while longer to get past the neuropathy, but that is a small price to pay, really. It was strange to walk into the office too after so much time away -and they even left my office in tact. I wouldn't have been surprised to have been moved to the "visiting consultant's" office either.

Autumn and I will head home this afternoon but it already is a good day. So yes, the sun is up, I'm vertical and the good day continues.

September 15th A.M.

Sep 15, 2014 6:11am

Life is defined as the animate existence or period of animate existence of an individual. We measure our lives from birth to death. But it is what we experience in between that helps define us. Each phase of our life is like a chapter in a book, from newborn, toddler, school age, teenager, young and then mature adult. Our loves help bring meaning to our life but don't define them. We define our life.

Likewise, the difficulties we face impact us, our loved ones, our families and our friends. This past fourteen months has brought a difficulty that I can't even imagine was before me when I first felt the pain in my groin and then the doctor's call that the test results were not good. Cancer is never a word, let alone a disease, that anyone expects to visit them. I certainly never expected that type of diagnosis. But like mad Madam Mimm in her sorcerer's duel with Merlin, Geoff, you've got it – Cancer.

My highs, and most of my lows, have been shared with the readers of this blog. The chapter in some ways is done as I am now "in remission". But in others, it will never be finished. Yes, I'm a cancer survivor, but I will never be the same. Friendships have been made, strengthened, others lost. I have a new found respect for the work done by caregivers, researchers and those working to make a cancer patient's life that much better.

My life will head in whatever direction lies before me, with my return to working (a bit more than I have fortunately but with limitations) helping others deal with the pain and suffering of cancer and trying to make the most of whatever life remains now that I am cancer free.

To everyone who has taken the time to read my musings from August 2013 through this one, thank you. Your Guestbook entries, Comments, e-mails, phone calls and HUGS have made this journey so much more tolerable (dare I almost say pleasant) that there will never be a way to thank each of you. The fact I haven't called, e-mailed or shown up on one's doorstep is not a slight on you but more a reflection of the vast number of people that reached out to help that it will take a long time to say thank you in person.

This blog isn't over by any means, but the chapter called having Cancer is fortunately closed.

And in case you are wondering,

"The sun is up, I'm vertical and it is a (very) good day".

GUESTBOOK (COMMENTS)

Sending you and Autumn many gentle hugs and thoughts of healing.

— Nancy Rapoport, August 26, 2013

My father gave me the greatest gift anyone could give me. He believed in me.

Daddy your the best father, friend, and business man I know. There is nothing that will change that and nothing can take away the strength that you have shown me and my sister day in and day out for 23 years of my short life.

We will make it through anything and I can't wait to have you by my side through the next phase of my life.

I love you so much and I made mom promise to give you extra kisses for me. I don't think it will be hard for her to hold up that bargain ;)

Michelle Berman, August 26, 2013

Hey Geoff and Autumn, thanks for setting this up so we can keep in touch without feeling that we may be intruding. Please let us know if we can help in any way. Our hearts and thoughts are with all of you. And we know that with your strength and grace you will all get through this challenge.

— Lynnette Warman, August 26, 2013

Keep thinking good thoughts and know that we are, as well. Love to you, Autumn and the family, Geoff.

— Ted Gavin, August 26, 2013

Sorry you are having to deal with this. You are a tough guy and I know will be able to overcome this hurdle. I will be praying for you and the family <3

— Adrienne Lindblad, August 26, 2013

Geoff,

Tackle this "case" as diligently and passionately as you always do, and I'm sure you will WIN!

Love and hugs from your family in O-HI-O ...

— Kathi Whitacre, August 26, 2013

Geoff,

Listen to the doctors and take care of yourself! Sending lots of love to all of you!

— Vicki Lawhorn, August 26, 2013

We will be thinking of you this week with positive thoughts and prayers. Take care of each other and we'll check in on your blog for your updates.

Hugs!

Lisa & Paul

— Lisa Stroube, August 26, 2013

Hey Geoff, I am thinking of you and praying for a speedy recovery. At least you have a great caretaker (Autumn) right by your side. Love you.

— Lisa Polizzi, August 27, 2013

Hang in there Geoff...keep thinking happy thoughts! Hugs to you and Autumn and try and get a good night's sleep :-)

— Lisa Stroube, August 27, 2013

I have the toughest strongest dad in the world. Nothing is stronger then you and our family. I love you.

— Michelle Berman, August 28, 2013

You're going to make it through this--and you and Autumn need but to call or email and we'll all help you guys!

— Nancy Rapoport, August 28, 2013

We've been through a number of adventures in our 30+ years of friendship. First, it was my turn; now it's yours.

You will be successful my friend, because I simply won't accept any other answer....

— Thomas Tone, August 28, 2013

Geoff,

Our thoughts, prayers and good "mojo" our out there for you, Autumn and the kids. In a few months this will all be behind you and you'll be out there chasing golf balls again in lovely palm springs.

Jim and Laura

— Jim Markus, August 29, 2013

Not spreading is good. Nurses et al saying "it's a Very Good Thing" means ... it's a VERY GOOD THING. Am heartened by the news!

— Nancy Rapoport, August 29, 2013

Geoff,

Encouraging news today!
Enjoy the weekend.
Expect good news early next week.
Love, hugs and good wishes to you and Autumn.

— Kathi Whitacre, August 29, 2013

Geoff glad to hear today was ok. You're right to stay positive and build on what you heard today.

Just know that you and Autumn are in Cindy's and my hearts and we have been praying for you.

All or love

Cindy and Bruce Nathan

— Bruce Nathan, August 29, 2013

Geoff -- Continuing to think about you, and Autumn, and sending you special thoughts each day. Especially now, when we are about to begin the holiday season, Wendy and I wish you only the best of health and happiness, and a sweet and prosperous New Year for you and the entire Berman family. Love and hugs from both of us. RICK

— Richard Meth, September 3, 2013

Sounds like a cautious so far so good. Sending you our best with fingers crossed!

— Lynnette Warman, September 3, 2013

Geoff:

You were in our prayers at temple today.

We know it will be a great new year for you and Autumn and your family and we hope to be a part of it.

All our love

Cindy and Bruce Nathan.

— Bruce Nathan
—, September 5, 2013

Geoff, VERY encouraging news to end the week. However, I'm sure everyone would agree the heart test was a waste. We already knew your heart is huge, warm and caring ... nothing wrong with it at all. I hope all goes well next week. Love and hugs to you and Autumn, and thanks for the updates.

— Kathi Whitacre, September 6, 2013

hi there; eyes are slanted, no hair, and stained his shirt.

— Norman Hanover, September 7, 2013

Geoff -- Here's to taking (and enjoying) things one day at a time, knowing how much you're cared about by friends, and how much you're loved by family. Wendy and I look forward to sharing one of those bottles you've placed on that newly built wine rack, together with many others, in the months and years ahead. In the meantime, now that you've been inscribed in the Book of Life, "be sealed, baby, be sealed." RICK & Wendy Meth

— Richard Meth, September 8, 2013

Geoff; thanks for the update; hug, hug, hug

Lulu & Norm

— Norman Hanover, September 9, 2013

Visited with Brianne this weekend as she is in her last year of her doctorate in PT at your old stomping ground, UOP. We were chatting about you and your family and our memories of Rutgers. We know how you execute plans and send our love and prayers for a clean bill of health! Sending you a BIG hug :)

— Adrienne Lindblad, September 9, 2013

I'm praying for you my friend and so is the cast of thousands I call my family.

— Thomas Tone, September 12, 2013

Glad to hear some very good news about your diagnosis!

— Nancy Rapoport, September 12, 2013

Glad to hear some positive news (not that anything about the dreaded C is good, but sometime not bad news = good news). Anyways, love that positive attitude and we keep thinking good thoughts and wishes for a full and healthy recovery.

Jim and L

— Jim Markus, September 12, 2013

This is great news Geoff
We extend our continuing love and support
Cindy and Bruce Nathan

— Bruce Nathan, September 13, 2013

Thinking of you

— Lisa Polizzi, September 13, 2013

Keeping up with your posts and happy to hear your voice. Stay positive and surround yourself with love from friends and family. Containment sounds like a good thing and hope that the logistical and bureaucratic issues get resolved quickly, so that you can heal quickly too! To all of the Berman family ... take care!

— Vicki Lawhorn, September 13, 2013

Geoff, Amy and I are thinking about you today as you start treatment. There is nothing, absolutely nothing, about this illness that is not lesser than you and there is nothing about you that is not exponentially greater than that which you are treating today. We and all of your friends and colleagues are with you.

— Ted Gavin, September 16, 2013

Geoff,

Six stars (on a five star scale) for your courage today!! Stay strong.

— Kathi Whitacre, September 16, 2013

Glad to hear it is ok so far. And a big congrats to the soon to be new grandparents!

— Lynnette Warman, September 17, 2013

Congrats on handling round 1 of your treatment, but a bigger congratulations to you and Autumn on soon to becoming grandparents! How exciting <3

— Adrienne Lindblad, September 17, 2013

I'm sending you and Autumn hugs (and a hearty mazel tov on the grandparent news)!

— Nancy Rapoport, September 18, 2013

Each day is a new "adventure" -- sometimes good, and sometimes not so much. But, so long as the sun comes up, you're surrounded and supported by those who care about you, and there are occasional bits of great news -- congrats on the wonderful news from Arielle and Ryan -- you've got all the motivation and "reasons" you need to keep going forward. And that I/we know you will, towards the desired end result. Thoughts and hugs to you, and to Autumn, from Wendy and me. RICK

— Richard Meth, September 18, 2013

You certainly have the right "attitude" to kick cancer's a--!!! Keep up the good work, hugs to you and Autumn from the Ohio family!!!

— Donna Gunn, September 19, 2013

Oh yeah, and being a grandparent is such fun! So happy for all of you!

— Donna Gunn, September 19, 2013

Thanks for the update.
When you feel like going out for a light (or heavy) dinner, call us.

Love, Lulu & Norm

— Norman Hanover, September 19, 2013

Way to go Bermans! Love the photo. I am so glad to hear that you are doing so well. One day at a time!

— Lynnette Warman, September 21, 2013

glad to hear the news; good that you went to the mixer; there is an Italian Heritage party on 10/3; starts at the bocce ball court at 4:30 and a barbecue follows about 6:30; if you want to go, let me know.

Norm

— Norman Hanover, September 21, 2013

Nice seeing you yesterday; just keep going one day at a time.

Norm

— Norman Hanover, September 23, 2013

We love you

Bruce and Cindy Nathan

— Bruce Nathan, September 23, 2013

I need to lose a few pounds as well, but if you don't mind, I'll try another way....

— Thomas Tone, September 26, 2013

Keep it up; enjoy your family, friends, and what God gives you each day.

— Norman Hanover, September 27, 2013

Hang in there and good luck tomorrow.

All our love

Bruce and Cindy Nathan

— Bruce Nathan, September 29, 2013

Still in Irvine and coming home tomorrow.

So sorry to hear you had a rough day. I'm sure tomorrow won't be easy but have Autumn let me know if I can be of any assistance. Take care and good luck tomorrow.

Hugs,

Lisa and Paul

— Lisa Stroube, September 29, 2013

Big day for you and the TanMan! Stay strong, keep us updated and we will do the same.

Incision was made at 9:10 am EST and will go late into the evening. Strong positive vibes coming your way!!!

— Donna Gunn, September 30, 2013

Just keep thinking that it will end at a certain point and hang in

All or love and support

Bruce and Cindy Nathan

— Bruce Nathan, September 30, 2013

Our best to you! Rest and relax today and give your body a chance to recoup some "normalcy." That convoy must have made it's way to Ohio, 'cause the Tan Man got run over yesterday too. "May the force be with you!!!"

— Donna Gunn, October 1, 2013

While I am fighting a miserable cold that has knocked me flat today, I know that you having a much worse time of it. My heart goes out to you, my friend.

— Thomas Tone, October 1, 2013

And another day is behind you.... Today was better than yesterday, and tomorrow will be better than today. And so the cycle continues, my friend. Even when we occasionally miss a day or two "signing in", rest assured that we're still always thinking of you and Autumn. Rick & Wendy

— Richard Meth, October 1, 2013

Hi Geoff.

I know you're feeling like you've been run over by a few deuce-and-a-half's right now and will be climbing out for the rest of the week. Know that my and Amy's thoughts are with you and Autumn.

No matter how discouraging this is; no matter how powerless or out of control of your own life you may feel; no matter how much you feel you need to step outside your box - please don't feel that you take it upon yourself to start a crystal meth empire. That would be bad.

Even though you might be able to pull off the porkpie hat. MIGHT be able to.

Now you go on about getting back to well, sir.

Much love,

— Ted Gavin, October 1, 2013

Geoff;

Please print out and save your daily updates; they will make a fine book for reading by others who face your problem, and it will give them the uplift they need to to get through each day, as you do, with hope and confidence that you will lick this problem, and go on to a better life and retirement.

The sun will continue to rise each day, and you are and will remain vertical.

Lulu & Norm

— Norman Hanover, October 2, 2013

Dear Geoff,

I like to write Haiku, in the 5/7/5 format. Here's one:

You'll be better soon (5)
And you'll still be plenty tall (7)
Everyone likes you. (5)

Yours,

David.

— David Meadows, October 3, 2013

You look darn good to us!

All our love

Bruce and Cindy Nathan

— Bruce Nathan, October 3, 2013

Actually, I like the look a lot! Signed, the Hug Mistress.....

— Nancy Rapoport, October 4, 2013

Geoff,

The front looks great. However, to be honest, the dark, flippy ponytail in the back seems a little extreme for such a classy guy. It needs to be thinned out because it looks like a moustache! :)

— Kathi Whitacre, October 4, 2013

Need new photo with the new look!

— Lynnette Warman, October 4, 2013

Geoff;

Your message is loud and clear; please, please keep a log and collect your writings. They are wonderful, insightful, and inspiring.

Lulu & Norm

— Norman Hanover, October 6, 2013

We are so glad that another round is behind you. One step closer to the finish line!

Now all you need is a black hat and shades and you can be Heisenberg for Halloween!

— Lynnette Warman, October 6, 2013

Love the message about living well each day. Thanks its a great reminder for all of us.

Wishing you well

Jim

— Jim Markus, October 7, 2013

Just checking in. Glad round #2 is behind you. Looking forward to seeing you soon. You are an incredible friend and mentor.

Talk soon.

Scott

— Scott Williams, October 8, 2013

Just wanted to e-mail and say we are thinking of you!

Bruce and Cindy Nathan

— Bruce Nathan, October 12, 2013

One step closer to chemo-free Mondays, Geoff. Get lots of rest and know you're in our thoughts.

— Ted Gavin, October 14, 2013

Hi Geoff,

Hope this week's treatment goes well and that the week goes by quickly!

Jim

— Jim Markus, October 14, 2013

Happy Columbus Day to you and Autumn. Good luck today!

> — Bruce Nathan, October 14, 2013

Halfway through Geoff!
That is a milestone.
Hang in there.

All our love

Bruce and Cindy

> — Bruce Nathan, October 15, 2013

Way to go Geoff and putting it in "D-women" swimming terms (this is for you Michelle) you are 825 yards through your 1650!

Great job and keep on keeping on.

Sending love and hugs to you and the family :)

> — Adrienne Lindblad, October 15, 2013

We are thinking of you; you are in our prayers; we will take you back to Georges so you can gain some more weight.

Love, Lulu & Norm

> — Norman Hanover, October 15, 2013

Geoff, Wrote you an email several weeks ago but I am not sure it went through. My best thoughts are with you and your family. You are probably not aware that I went through surgery and chemo last year and am now on the other side of it.

Glad that you are 1/2 way through it -- I counted every time (started in April and ended in

August). There is another side and it is so nice to be here. I certainly hope never to do all of this again and hope that once you get through this you will not have to either. Take care of yourself. Hope you will be at a point where you can go to WLC. Best,

— Deborah Thorne, October 15, 2013

I can imagine how tough days like this are, and I'm glad that you and Autumn are each other's touchstones. Sending you hugs galore.

— Nancy Rapoport, October 16, 2013

I love your positive attitude!

— Donna Gunn, October 19, 2013

Keep up the good fight; I am not as articulate as you but we pray for you each day and know that you will be healthy soon, as well as vertical.

Love, Lulu and Norm

— Norman Hanover, October 21, 2013

I can only imagine how scary it was to pass out--ye of maximum ability to control most things--and I'm so glad that you and Autumn are there for each other. Hugs, the HugMaster

— Nancy Rapoport, October 21, 2013

As usual, you have a way with words that makes the story even better. To repeat myself, be sure you are keeping your entries in a journal, which, after you are cured, as the final entry, would easily be published for all cancer patients, their family and friends and the general public to read and understand what the "patient" is going thru day by day. It would be required reading at the chemo center.

Norm

— Norman Hanover, October 23, 2013

Those are some great pics and it sounds like a super organization!

— Scott Williams, October 24, 2013

Fabulous photos! You both look fantastic and at peace with all that is going on. I shared it on Facebook so that some of the ABI folks can see it as well. Amy and Ted shared it as well, so you are definitely getting some great coverage! What a fun idea.

— Lynnette Warman, October 24, 2013

Geoff and Autumn, you brightened my day today. Thank you for the phone call. It was so good to hear your voice and catch up. You're amazing! Love you both!

— Amy Gavin, October 24, 2013

You look great, Geoff. I mean, there isn't a part of me that doesn't want to scream and break something, but seeing you look that good is the high point in a month that hasn't treated a lot of good people well. I miss you, sir.

— Ted Gavin, October 24, 2013

I am inspired by your courage and openness. Our thoughts and prayers are with you, your wonderful wife and daughters. Love, Felicia Turner Burda and Family

— Felicia Burda, October 25, 2013

Thanks for the link to your modeling gig - both you and Autumn look fabulous! Sending positive thoughts, hugs and blessings your way.

— Adrienne Lindblad, October 25, 2013

It is truly amazing what you discover in this world when a tragedy such as a serious health issue arises. None of us ever heard of the work that Debbie and her crew does before you became a cancer patient. it just shows that although we think we are "up to date" on the world, and its surroundings, we really are in the dark about some things that help brighten the days of people facing serious problems.

Thanks for educating us.

Norm

— Norman Hanover, October 26, 2013

I just read your posts for the past week and saw all your pictures. Consider changing your career to modeling; the pictures show a different side of you!

Enjoy the weekend and good luck for the upcoming week.

Bruce and Cindy!

— Bruce Nathan, October 26, 2013

Geoff Berman

Geoff:

The pitcher for the Red Sox, who beat St. Louis last night, recovered from a non-Hodgkin's lymphoma. They announced it during the game.

Also, there is a comedy show on February 19 at Sun City, the second one; the first was great; I have tickets, and have reserved several on either side of ours; let me know when you are ready, and I will save two for you and Autumn.

Meanwhile, as always, we are praying for you.

Lulu & Norm

— Norman Hanover, October 29, 2013

Geoff,

High five on the encouraging test results! It's so very good to hear this. Hugs and candy kisses (in celebration of Halloween) to you and Autumn.

— Kathi Whitacre, October 31, 2013

Never thought I'd root for necrosis, but in this context, YAY!

— Nancy Rapoport, October 31, 2013

So glad to hear that the treatments are working and thanks for keeping us so well-informed about the chemo roller coaster.

Keep fighting!!

Jim

— Jim Markus, October 31, 2013

Great news!! With a grandchild in your future this news is awesome!!! p.s. the TanMan says he hopes it's a boy!!!

— Donna Gunn, October 31, 2013

Thank g-d for the favorable test results.

May they continue to be favorable so you can rid yourself of the interloper and return your life to you and Autumn.

Cindy and I continue to pray for you and send all our love!

— Bruce Nathan, November 2, 2013

So very good to hear your voice the other day. I gave an update to Wendy and she -- like I -- are so very pleased that things appear to be progressing so well. Keep up "the good work"!

Also have to admit that I'm a bit jealous as to how good you look without hair. Quite classic -- and, dare I say, strikingly handsome -- my friend. Keep on keepin' on...

RICK (and Wendy)

— Richard Meth, November 5, 2013

I love you dad <3

— Michelle Berman, November 6, 2013

Just know that all of us love you and are sending you "you will kick cancer's butt" thoughts.

Hugs, The Hugger

— Nancy Rapoport, November 6, 2013

and thank you for sharing with us.

We love and support you and Autumn

B and C Nathan

> — Bruce Nathan, November 6, 2013

Again, your blog is easy to read, informative, and not at all negative. Your mind set makes sure you will recover full health, and enjoy life to it fullest.

Norm

> — Norman Hanover, November 11, 2013

Your picture looks darn good! Hang in there!

Bruce and Cindy

> — Bruce Nathan, November 11, 2013

Save a seat on the bus for us. Lulu says she saw both of you walking yesterday. Fabulous.

Lulu & Norm

> — Norman Hanover, November 13, 2013

Angie says hello, best wishes, and thanks for thinking of him. He obviously thinks a lot of you! Glad to hear things are going so well. Take care.

> — Lynnette Warman, November 15, 2013

Geoff;

Got you message; as usual, glad to hear from hear you. Seems like you are well on your way to recovery.

Just a coincidence, but someone else has a birthday Tuesday, Her name is Lulu; at this time of the year she changes to Polish, as it is celebrated for almost a week between her friends and her kids. Wish Autumn a great birthday, and a 300 game as a present.

Norm.

— Norman Hanover, November 17, 2013

Oh, forgot to congratulate you on the holes in one. Join the Couples Putters next Saturday, and we can play together for the first week.

Norm

— Norman Hanover, November 17, 2013

It is a good day; Autumn and Lulu share another candle on their cake, and we are thankful for all that we have.

— Norman Hanover, November 19, 2013

Hope all goes well; see if you can "duck" when the "whack" comes your way

Norm

— Norman Hanover, November 20, 2013

Ah, thanks for mentioning me in your blog...I feel quite special! :-)

I thought the sentiment fitted you perfectly as you two really are there for each other every day.

Today is round 5, a difficult one to be sure, but one that brings you closer to the end of this part of the journey. Good luck today...and when you get home you can be lulled asleep by beautiful music from your newly (and finally) installed Bose system!

Stay strong!

Lisa

— Lisa Stroube, November 20, 2013

Lulu and I have long supported the Desert Cancer Foundation, which provides medical treatment for cancer patients and also the local chapter of Gilda's Club, which has offices in Cathedral City, and does a magnificent job in support for the families of cancer patients. They do a great job in aiding local people. If anyone needs addresses, please let me know.

Geoff; warm up your putter, as we look forward to giving you a lesson tomorrow.

Lulu & Norm

— Norman Hanover, November 22, 2013

You're looking good kid!
And getting closer to the bogie!
We continue to send our love and keep you in our prayers to beat this darn thing!

Bruce and Cindy Nathan

— Bruce Nathan, November 22, 2013

No putting next week, but Lulu and I may want a rematch soon. Good fun, good friends, good time.

Lulu & Norm

— Norman Hanover, November 23, 2013

May your Thanksgiving day be full of family, good cheer, good food, and thanks for what we have.

You will return to good health, and are an inspiration to us all.

Love, Lulu & Norm

— Norman Hanover, November 27, 2013

Happy thanksgiving to you, Autumn and your family!

Cindy and Bruce Nathan

— Bruce Nathan, November 27, 2013

So glad you all had a Happy Thanksgiving! The Tan Man stayed away from the cranberry sauce and chose pureed bananas and peas instead. As an extended family we have so much to be thankful for this year! Best wishes to you all.

— Donna Gunn, December 1, 2013

I don't know if "enjoy" is the right description, but I enjoy reading your blogs. You may have missed your calling, as writing seems to become you, even though the subject is not the most pleasant one.

You may have to promise us you will keep it up through a a different medium after you "beat" this nasty illness.

Yes, the sun is up, it is a beautiful day, and that is because you help make it so.

Lulu & Norm

— Norman Hanover, December 1, 2013

We all succeed and fail on a daily basis. The best we can do is succeed more often. f we recognize this, as you have, the failures make the successes that much more sweet. When you succeed in becoming cancer free, the sweetness will be indescribable.

Lulu & Norm

— Norman Hanover, December 2, 2013

It's totally ok to be human. The nice thing about being loved--truly loved--is that your loved ones are ok w/the fact that you're not going to be perfect all the time. (Jeff is SO used to that about me!) The tricky thing for your loved ones is that they might be afraid to call you on your non-perfect-ness during, well, your non-perfect-ness, which makes them bottle up their feelings, too. So clearing the air from time to time helps all around. Hugs, The Hugger

— Nancy Rapoport, December 2, 2013

Best furry tree decorations ever!

— Nancy Rapoport, December 4, 2013

So glad that things keep moving along with relative ease. This will soon pass and you will be back with all of us at ABI events soon. I will be a very happy camper on that day.

— Lynnette Warman, December 4, 2013

Geoff,

I kind of like the bald look on you! Like your boots, not everyone can pull that off as well as you can. When you stand up now, taller than most of us, you probably are even more imposing than you were with a head of hair!

Your posts all carry the same positive, thoughtful attitude I associate with you, for all these years, but more than that. I note that every one of the posts have something to do with thinking about others. I'll always be grateful for the good thoughts over the years that you have sent my way.

Hang in there. You plainly are. And I agree with you -- it IS cold out!

— David Meadows, December 6, 2013

Yes, it's cold; I left for a meeting this morning at 7:am, bright sun and 37 degrees. got home at 10:30, 55 degrees.

Yes, time to count blessings. and yes, Happy Birthday to all and to all a good, healthy,, and happy year.

Lulu & Norm

— Norman Hanover, December 6, 2013

Sometimes baby steps are best.

You will get there my friend!

Love Bruce and Cindy

— Bruce Nathan, December 7, 2013

The desert is replete with great things to do without spending a lot of money. You and Autumn are finding out why this is a great place to live. You are also finding out that there is tremendous poverty in the east end of the valley, and their needs go on year around, not just at holiday time.

Although not Catholic (Lulu is) the work done by Father Lincoln for the families in Coachella and Mecca is a blessing. He takes up collections of money, food, clothing, and anything else that he can for those families year round. He raised money to build the church in Mecca, and spends lots of time there ministering to the needs of the people. He is blessed.

Keep exploring the desert, keep up your spirit, and when you "beat" this thing, we shall all have a big celebration.

Happy holidays,

Lulu & Norm

— Norman Hanover, December 9, 2013

And don't get down; the insurance carrier isn't god, and the need for the scan can't be ignored.

Future treatment depends on its results. So, scream, shout, and do whatever you can to embarrass the clerk (or jerk) who is reviewing your situation to realize what needs to be done.

Lulu & Norm

— Norman Hanover, December 11, 2013

Loved your blog today Geoff although truth be told, I enjoy them everyday. I watched the video and was very moved. I have heard a lot about the Jimmy V Foundation and is was nice to listen to his speech. What a great example of strength and optimism...as are you! Can't believe the insurance company is still being a "jerk". It's not easy to be a pawn in their administrative boondoggle...give 'em hell! Excuse my French :-)

Good luck today with your last whack-a-mole (or however you spell it). Sending a big hug to you and Autumn!

— Lisa Stroube, December 11, 2013

My former boss (very gruff and blunt surgeon) used to call the insurance company clerks "Diary Queen Dropouts." They're making their decisions based on a written a script of guidelines. Many of the insurance companies play a stalling game. You may have to take off your patient hat and put on your lawyer hat at some point. I'd love to be a fly on the wall for that conversation. Love your posts!

— Donna Gunn, December 12, 2013

Good to talk to you yesterday. It will be better to talk to you once you've crossed the finish line. We're all here cheering you on.

— Mark Berman, December 13, 2013

Hi Geoff. My first time on this website. I like it, and I like your posts. Keep them coming.

Very sorry about the insurance trouble. As your lawyer, I advise you to keep yelling.

— Paul Geilich, December 13, 2013

As usual your writing ability transcends the issues you face. You should publish all of your blogs under the name, One Day at a Time, days in the life of cancer patient or something like that.

I too have neuropathy in my left leg; it never goes away, and is a constant reminder of my treatment of my non-malignant tumor. I know how you feel, and I hope you are right that yours is temporary.

If you are up to it, lets go to dinner; Chef George awaits.

Love, Lulu & Norm,

— Norman Hanover, December 14, 2013

I know that you're in good hands w/your doc, and that although waiting to come "all the way back" early in the year won't happen, when you ARE back, you'll savor it that much more. We love you.

— Nancy Rapoport, December 14, 2013

This has been a crazy week; just read your posts for the week.
Sounds like 2 steps forward one step back.
Bottom line sounds like you are headed in the right direction and you are going to BEAT this thing.

And we are right behind you with our support and love.
Best thing is so is your loving family and your great network of friends.

Love Bruce and Cindy Nathan

— Bruce Nathan, December 15, 2013

Our days are easier to face because of your blogs; your ability to describe where you are and how you feel is inspiring to those of us who also have problems, which pale in light of yours.

Lulu & Norm

— Norman Hanover, December 16, 2013

Dr. Hug prescribes a belly laugh at least once a day. (If only Dr. Hug were funny and could tell jokes--her only joke is "How many psychiatrists does it take to change a light bulb? One, but the bulb really has to want to change....")

Hugs,

The Hugger

— Nancy Rapoport, December 16, 2013

Hang in there Geoff. In the grand scheme of things, it is just a small step backwards.

— Lynnette Warman, December 16, 2013

Geoff, you are a great role model of strength and courage. Hang in there- we are all here with you- and look forward to your treatment completion! Love Robbin and Barry

— Robbin Itkin, December 17, 2013

Geoff,

Happy holiday to you, Autumn and your family.

— Bruce Nathan, December 22, 2013

Jeff, every day you battle this thing is one day closer to a full cure. And the nice thing is you have lots of loving family and friends to draw support from. We are all here for you and love you. Happy holiday.

Bruce and Cindy Nathan

— Bruce Nathan, December 23, 2013

Enjoy the warmth of family and friends, Geoff. You're a rich man on both counts.

— Mark Berman, December 24, 2013

Merry Christmas and healthy and happy 2014.

— Bruce Nathan, December 24, 2013

Geoff and Autumn, I really wish the left coast extended family could see how much Tanner's (Tan Man) smile lights up the room. We are blessed to have him as one of the miracles of modern medicine. Your impending cure will also be one of those miraculous stories. Keep fighting the fight.....you'll have your own little one to light up the room next Christmas. What have I learned from you and the Tan Man? 1.) Never ever take life or health for granted. 2.) Never ever think it won't happen to you. 3.) A career doesn't hold a candle to family. My priorities are vastly different than they were a year ago thanks to a little guy with born with "half a heart." Have a blessed holiday season!!!!

— Donna Gunn, December 24, 2013

Glad to hear that you enjoyed a great Christmas with your family. Cindy and I wish you a happy and ultimate cancer free 2014.

— Bruce Nathan, December 28, 2013

Lulu and I wish you the very best for the New Year. It will be better than 2013, and when you return to good health you can look back and say you are the better for this awful experience because you have recognized the troubles many go through in silence.
See you next year.

Lulu & Norm

— Norman Hanover, December 31, 2013

New Year's was quiet, got bleary eyed watching football, but didn't learn anything, so will watch again tonight, and so on, pray for a better year for you and yours, and move on day by day

Lulu & Norm

— Norman Hanover, January 2, 2014

Geoff Berman

Thanks again for the insight to combat this terrible disease. Be sure you publish that to the others who also may be fighting it.

Lulu & Norm

— Norman Hanover, January 3, 2014

Keep fighting the good fight. Consider your many friends your army in this battle, happy to follow and support their General into the fray and onward towards victory. Here's to a HEALTHY 2014!

RICK & Wendy

— Richard Meth, January 3, 2014

Here's hoping that today is a better day.
Look forward to catching up this week.

— Bruce Nathan, January 5, 2014

Autumn now is a professional bowler and golfer. What is she going to take up next; can Bocce have professionals?

We are so happy that you and Autumn have found new activities, new friends, and are enjoying your move here in spite of the cancer that so unfairly attacked you at the time of the move.

Stay on the path to good health.

Fondly

Lulu & Norm

— Norman Hanover, January 5, 2014

If there is a bright light before the end of the tunnel, it is that you are able to walk the track and play bocce, make new friends, and have some time for yourself. I know that is something that you weren't able to do before this terrible disease hit you.

When you are cancer free, you will still be able to enjoy the walks, the bocce, and the putting and be full of life and new friends.

Norm

— Norman Hanover, January 9, 2014

Congrats to your mom. Obviously good genes run in your family. That is wonderful!

So sorry you will miss the party but some things can't be helped. Let's hope this last session really has that nasty cancer on its last legs!

— Lynnette Warman, January 11, 2014

Guess what; your mom will appreciate your thoughts, and I am sure a phone call will make her day, while staying home will be in your best interests, which is all that matters now.

Lulu & Norm.

— Norman Hanover, January 11, 2014

Happy 90th to your mom.
You are with her in her heart and yours too!

— Bruce Nathan, January 11, 2014

Wishing your mom a very, VERY happy 90th!

> — Nancy Rapoport, January 11, 2014

Are you walking around in your boots? I'd take that as a good sign, if you are. Glad to see your continuing positive attitude. Yet another of your fine features.

> — David Meadows, January 15, 2014

Another day as you move closer to good health; the only way we can help is pray with you and for you, so as I am sure you know that is what Lulu and I are doing.

Lulu & Norm.

> — Norman Hanover, January 15, 2014

I know how strong you and your family are Geoff. We are thinking of you all and sending positive thoughts and prayers. I am flying down to PD next Saturday (25th) to settle Eric's parents in their condo. I would love to see you and Autumn if you are up to it. Let me know. <3

> — Adrienne Lindblad, January 16, 2014

Oh man! That was not the news I was hoping to hear. The good part is that it sounds like the extended plan will be successful in the end. We have to keep an eye on the prize, as they say.

Sending you all positive thoughts and love.

Lynnette & Angelo

> — Lynnette Warman, January 16, 2014

Yes, keep your head down, be sure and take a full turn, and hit it straight down the fairway, so that all you will have is a chip shot home.

Line up the putt, and watch for the break. When the radiation is over, it is straight in the hole.

Lulu & norm

— Norman Hanover, January 16, 2014

I know it's not at all fun, what you're about to endure, but I do know many, many people for whom this worked really well. Pulling for you! Hugs, N.

— Nancy Rapoport, January 17, 2014

Geoff, good luck today. My thoughts will be with you, and they will be positive. Fight and endure, brother.

— Paul Geilich, January 20, 2014

It's nice to have a plan that provides a solution, even if it is a difficult plan to implement. Our hearts go out to you and we are thinking good thoughts your way every day. Too bad we can't wish that cancer away. Love you guys.

— Lynnette Warman, January 20, 2014

In honor of Geoff Berman.

— Amy Goldman, January 20, 2014

Geoff - Although we can't be with you in person, your family in Ohio is sending our love and support your way. Thanks to Autumn for being "The Rock." Hugs to both of you. Kathi

— Kathi Whitacre, January 20, 2014

Not much to say other than our prayers are still with you.

Lulu & Norm

— Norman Hanover, January 24, 2014

Geoff, boy at least there is some good news in all of this. I can't imagine what was going through Autumn and your heads when the spot showed up. Must be a good sign for you both...

— Thomas Tone, January 25, 2014

I just got back from China (incredibly successful trip) and look forward to catching up soon

All our love

— Bruce Nathan, January 25, 2014

Good news about the spot. Must have been scary for a while, but you can now just go forward with what needs to be done.

— Norman Hanover, January 26, 2014

Geoff,

Thanks for the good news about "the spot". May the meds quickly beat it into submission as you keep progressing forward towards your ultimate goal.

Wendy and I continue to send our thoughts and hugs your way. RICK

— Richard Meth, January 26, 2014

Sleep well.

You got me in the mood for a grilled cheese sandwich. Ah well I am going to bed too to get off China time and resume a northeastern lifestyle.

Hang in in there my friend.

— Bruce Nathan, January 27, 2014

What a day you had--I feel for you!

— Nancy Rapoport, January 27, 2014

Glad to hear your sense of humor remains intact. Reminds me of an old saying, "He who laughs lasts".

How is Arielle? Any news about the baby? Any thoughts of names? Nice to have something to look forward to.

— Lynnette Warman, January 27, 2014

Miss you, and so does Chef George. His volume is off and he needs the business.

When are you coming home? We have been practicing our putting and want a rematch.

Feel better, you are always in our prayers,

Fondly, Lulu & Norm

— Norman Hanover, January 27, 2014

Very good news, Geoff. Glad to hear about your good day. I like the photo, too.

— Paul Geilich, January 28, 2014

Great news my friend.

Enjoy the warmer weather while we on the east coast freeze!

All our love and support!

— Bruce Nathan, January 28, 2014

We will pick you up at six; we have many choices, so tell us where you would like to go; one thing I am good at is eating.

Norm

— Norman Hanover, January 30, 2014

Here's to being closer to getting rid of the interloper.

All the best my friend

— Bruce Nathan, January 30, 2014

So glad to hear that you're home, Geoff. Spent a bit of time catching up on your journal entries and encouraged to read that you're in the great hands of the City of Hope. Here's to vertical!

Give our best to Autumn too ... sorry to hear about her mom. Love to all of you!

— Vicki Lawhorn, January 31, 2014

Hey there. I've been a bit under the weather this week. Will call this weekend. Glad you get to be home for a while. The best place to rest and de-stress. Lots of love and positive thoughts your way!

Lynnette & Angelo

— Lynnette Warman, January 31, 2014

Happy to see so much love on this for my Dad! He is the best person I know, the best father a girl could ever ask for, and the best role model I have in my life. Love you so much Dad!!!! <3

— Michelle Berman, January 31, 2014

You mean like this? http://www.youtube.com/watch?v=w0ffwDYo00Q Hugs, N.

— Nancy Rapoport, February 1, 2014

Gosh, what next? Just the thought of those IV's has me quaking. Not my favorite either.

What are you doing to pass the time? Reading? Music? Need any books? We are pulling for you!

— Lynnette Warman, February 5, 2014

Just be happy you are not here on the east coast. The weather is driving us CRAZY!

Hang in there; each day brings you closer to the end of this lousy odyssey.

— Bruce Nathan, February 5, 2014

Sending you anti-pneumonia hugs!

— Nancy Rapoport, February 7, 2014

Finally some really good news!!!

— Thomas Tone, February 8, 2014

Very positive report on the road to a full recovery
We pray for only positive news to come.

— Bruce Nathan, February 8, 2014

Wahoo! It is really on the ropes now.

— Lynnette Warman, February 8, 2014

So pleased to hear the news about the PET scan results. Keep the good news coming, and keep up the good fight. You've got lots of "troops" behind you.

Best, RICK and Wendy

— Richard Meth, February 9, 2014

Excellent news about the PET scan, Geoff. I am so glad to hear it. Beautiful!

Paul

— Paul Geilich, February 10, 2014

Brother,

http://youtu.be/rOPDhoZH91g
We can do this.
Fight On!

Ricardo

— Richard Meyer, February 11, 2014

Nothing new to report here; where is Autumn? If she is around, let us know so we can take her out to dinner, or whatever.

— Norman Hanover, February 12, 2014

Missed seeing you in person yesterday but glad you were on the phone.

Hang in there!

— Bruce Nathan, February 13, 2014

So glad you are home and can get some real rest! There is no place like home.

— Lynnette Warman, February 15, 2014

Great news on your getting home. Here's to an up trajectory towards a full cure.

— Bruce Nathan, February 15, 2014

Welcome back to heaven; the sun is shining, and it is great to be here. Give us a call when you are ready to eat.

Love to Autumn, and you to. We watch with awe your strength and determination.

Lulu & Norm

— Norman Hanover, February 15, 2014

Welcome home, sir! Glad to hear it.

— Paul Geilich, February 17, 2014

There is no place like home!

— Lynnette Warman, February 17, 2014

Thanks for sharing the good news. Helped to bring some sunshine into a cloudy and, yes, occasionally snowy, day. Even when we're "quiet" we're thinking of you and sending good vibes and virtual hugs your (and Autumn's) way.

RICK and Wendy

— Richard Meth, February 26, 2014

I'm glad to see you are recovering from the pneumonia, I'm sorry you got it. This last year has been so special with our grandson (he'll be one next Thursday), and I cannot wait for both you and Autumn to experience being a grandparent. As much as I love my children and was so excited for their births, a grandchild is something you cannot explain. Please let us know when Arielle has the baby, and good luck with your treatments.

I'm glad to see you've kept your sense of humor, it is probably the one single most important thing in your full recovery. God Bless you both and I'm glad to see you're up for the fight and surrender is NOT an option.

— Peter Baccaro, February 27, 2014

The rain will bring flowers to brighten your day.

— Norman Hanover, February 28, 2014

Great to hear about Arielle and something wonderful to look forward to Grandpa Geoff (and Grandma Autumn).

You both have a beautiful grandchild to look forward to and lavish lots of love over.

We love you both

Bruce and Cindy

PS

Better your rain than our snow and frigidly cold arctic temperatures. Stay dry.

— Bruce Nathan, February 28, 2014

it is always a good day when we read that you are on the right road, and that you had fun over the weekend.

Lulu & Norm

— Norman Hanover, March 3, 2014

What a relief--things are getting back on track again. Looks like the shower went well and everyone is healthy and happy. Can't wait to see the photos with the baby!

— Lynnette Warman, March 5, 2014

Geoff,

68 / 80

It's so great to see Pat and Arielle together... Thanks so much for sharing the photo... However, they both look so young! I think I'll stay away from mirrors for a while! I look like Methuselah compared to those two chicks!

Ricardo

— Richard Meyer, March 5, 2014

Beautiful picture; glad you and Autumn were able to enjoy. And the best is yet to come.

BN

— Bruce Nathan, March 5, 2014

It is a long process, and it has to wear on you.

if you are available this week, let's go have a dinner and talk again as we do.

Love, Lulu & norm

— Norman Hanover, March 11, 2014

I love that last post and have had the donor acknowledgment on my license as long as I can remember. Not to diminish Geoff's message but to expand on it, there are a number of ways we can help each other, become a member of the bone marrow registry, or donate platelet's and plasma through the Red Cross. If you want to know more, go to http://redcrossblood.org/donating-blood/types-donations/platelets. Different than whole blood donations, you can donate every two weeks and they desperately need people willing to make the commitment. I have been doing it for approximately 15 years with over 300 donations and it is the best two hours I will ever spend. It has happened less than six times, but when they tell you your platelets are going on a plane for a matching patient as soon as the donation is over, no greater feeling.

— Peter Baccaro, March 13, 2014

As always our thoughts, prayers and love is with you and your family Geoff. Your strength and positive attitude is truly amazing and inspirational. Looking forward to seeing you next time I make it to the desert.

— Adrienne Lindblad, March 13, 2014

We read your blogs like we read the daily newspaper. We won't get up at 4:00am either, unless we have to urinate.

Lulu and Norm

— Norman Hanover, March 13, 2014

The surprise party was fun, and we still got there a little early. It was at Jillian's, and it is the cat's meow. Thought you might like that description. It is a place you go to on special occasions and we will go there to celebrate your completion of your stem cell procedures.

Be well; our prayers are with you

Lulu & Norm

— Norman Hanover, March 16, 2014

Geoff:

Thanks for the faithful updates. Makes me feel better to know that you are getting such great care. I can't wait to celebrate the end of this journey and your return to good health!

Big hugs!

— Lynnette Warman, March 16, 2014

Wahoo! You were due for some good news. Let's hope it's the start of a good trend to the end do the treatment!

— Lynnette Warman, March 19, 2014

Another hurdle successfully surmounted and another to go. Wow, you can see the light at the end of the tunnel.

We're with you!

Love Cindy and Bruce

— Bruce Nathan, March 20, 2014

The sun is rising and with it is a new day that will bring you closer to the successful result of this awful journey. No one who hasn't been there can really understand or feel what you are going through, but we can and do pray for you each day.

Lulu & Norm

— Norman Hanover, March 25, 2014

Kind of missing Hawaii too. Am busy tending to my son. He is recovering from a ruptured patellar tendon and can't do much for himself for while. Glad his pain is beginning to dissipate.

— Lynnette Warman, March 25, 2014

Just know that we love you guys.

— Nancy Rapoport, March 25, 2014

Happy Anniversary Geoff and Autumn! Here's to 31 more years together <3

— Adrienne Lindblad, March 26, 2014

Sending you both anniversary hugs!

Signed,

The Hugger

— Nancy Rapoport, March 26, 2014

Our 32nd anniversary is Friday; next year we will have a great celebration together.

Lulu & Norm

— Norman Hanover, March 26, 2014

First happy 31st anniversary to Autumn and you. What a milestone and what a special couple you are. We hope there are many anniversaries to come with good health and much happiness!

Ok so you are heading into the final phase of the fight. WE look forward to the next time we see you cancer free and full of wisdom, fun and love.

Bruce and Cindy

— Bruce Nathan, March 29, 2014

Lulu and I would love to donate blood, but we can't; we agree that it is a wonderful thing to help others.

We look forward to tonight's date for dinner, and will pick you up at 5:45;

Lulu and Norm

— Norman Hanover, March 29, 2014

Good luck, Geoff ... and goodbye cancer. We think of you every day. Stay strong and feel better soon. Jerry and I are counting on you and Autumn to represent the grandparents at the big event!! Love ya.

— Kathi Whitacre, March 31, 2014

Go for it, Geoff! We're all there rooting for you, and for Autumn and the girls. Here's to new beginnings...

HUGS from Rick & Wendy

— Richard Meth, March 31, 2014

Your strength and family support are inspirations for all of us! Let the final battle of this long struggle begin!

— Lynnette Warman, March 31, 2014

Slay the dragon, sir. I KNOW you will. I'm so glad your ordeal is almost over.

— Paul Geilich, March 31, 2014

YEAH!!! So glad to hear the news!
Way to go my friend

Jim

— Jim Markus, March 31, 2014

See, the food at Jackalope must have done it.
Best of wishes; good luck, and all that

Love, Lulu & Norm

— Norman Hanover, March 31, 2014

So happy for all of you!

— Lynnette Warman, March 31, 2014

Geoff - Wonderful news! I pray the next few days fly by so you can move on to the final leg of this long journey. I can't wait to hear from you again.

Love to you and Autumn

— Terri Steinbrenner, March 31, 2014

I am thrilled at your news.
I am also happy that I just figured out how to sign in on this site.

— Stephen Darr, March 31, 2014

Outstanding! Amazing!

— Paul Geilich, March 31, 2014

So thankful for the great news Geoff! We are keeping you all in our thoughts and prayers. In swimmer terms, you are at the 60th lap of the mile! Cheers to remission and a complete recovery!

— Adrienne Lindblad, March 31, 2014

Geoff -- Thanks for sharing the wonderful news! Wendy and I continue to root for you, sending HUGS and all other sorts of good vibes and wishes. Here's to victory at the end of the home stretch.

Keep on keepin' on... RICK & Wendy

— Richard Meth, March 31, 2014

Your chronicles are testament of your positive spirit and stamina and I'm thrilled to hear that your journey is now on the bell lap! Bring it home strong, my friend! Love to you and Autumn and the girls, and that little grandbaby on his way.

— Vicki Lawhorn, March 31, 2014

Whoo-hooo! YAY!

Hugs,

The Hugger

— Nancy Rapoport, April 1, 2014

Incredibly wonderful news!!!!

— Donna Gunn, April 1, 2014

You're a wonderful man and we all care deeply about you and your family.

— Stephen Darr, April 1, 2014

How absolutely fabulous!!

— Lynnette Warman, April 8, 2014

Such a great picture of a wonderful group of people... even that blond in the red shirt playing with your leg :-)

Sorry to hear about the virus and having to extend your vacation. We'll look forward to having you back in the windy desert early next week.

Feel better!

Hugs,

Lisa and Paul

— Lisa Stroube, April 25, 2014

A fantastic service to the patient and his or her loved ones!

— Thomas Tone, April 29, 2014

CPSIA information can be obtained at www.ICGtesting.com
Printed in the USA
BVOW04s1915010415

394355BV00004B/26/P

9 781504 328289